Wilbur's Trave

Travelling by Train Across the Balkans

A HORNBILL PUBLISHING BOOK

First published in the UK in 2019
by Hornbill Publishing

Copyright © Will Linsdell
www.wilburstravels.com

All rights reserved. This book or any portion thereof may not be reproduced or used in any manner whatsoever without the express written permission of the author, except for brief quotations in a book review.

ISBN 9781797552903

Published by Hornbill Publishing, London, UK.

Cover Photo – Stari Most, Mostar, Bosnia & Herzegovina

WARNING

This book may appear to contain stereotypes. However, every account I give is an unbiased & accurate reflection of what I experienced.

"I dislike feeling at home when I am abroad."

George Bernard Shaw

For Rania

Contents

Introduction

The Balkans – A Brief History

Chapter 1 – A Short Balkan Interlude

Chapter 2 – Byzantine

Chapter 3 – A Tale of Three Cities

Chapter 4 – No Beards

Chapter 5 – The Former Yugoslavia

Chapter 6 – Old Town Rules

Chapter 7 – So Near, Sofia

Chapter 8 – Slovenian Sojourn

Chapter 9 – Many Happy Returns

Chapter 10 – Action Stations

Bonus Chapter – Balkan Holidays

Picture Gallery

Reflections

Glossary of Terms

Dark Beer Ratings

Balkan Train Journeys

About the Author

Coming Next

Introduction

This book is the first instalment chronicling the travels, triumphs & trials of me Wilbur (Will), and Hamish (aka Earos), my regular travel companion, as we explored Eastern Europe & Eurasia over the past decade or two.

Friends since senior school, we never tire of planning the next trip, a trip that will invariably include cross-border train travel.

Our rail journeys started in 1992 with the gift of inter-rail (a bargain unlimited monthly European rail pass, as it was at the time). The inclination back then was to cram in as much as possible into three to four weeks, new experience after new experience, a railroad to heaven.

Over a decade later, circumstance saw us re-enact this spirit with what were to become pretty much annual pilgrimages.

The trips may be slightly less frenetic and a little more luxurious than they were in those adolescent days of the early '90s, but exactly the same magic, intrigue and all-to-common perplexing moments are still conjured on a regular basis.

Read about our own remarkable experiences, hilarious mishaps and the myriad of eccentric characters that we met along the way.

The Allure of Eastern European Train Travel – An Excerpt:

'The five of us had all run out of food, conversation and any inspiration by the time we finally crawled into Sofia an excruciating six hours late. 163km in just under ten hours.

17km per hour average speed, when you consider the hours spent standing idle in freezing conditions as the driver and train guard tried to fix the heating and lighting armed with just a screwdriver, some pliers and zero electrical skills.

The train still had to get to Istanbul, another 550 km further east. We felt really sorry for the two unsuspecting old ladies that we saw board as we alighted. At this rate it could be days before they reached Turkey! There was no sign of any qualified heating engineers either.

At this stage I had not noticed that Hamish was showing early signs of hypothermia……………'

WE WOULDN'T HAVE IT ANY OTHER WAY!

The Balkans – A Brief History

This book is set in the Balkan Peninsular, an area stretching from west to east from Slovenia to Istanbul, also taking in all the former Yugoslav countries, Albania, Bulgaria and Northern Greece.

Some authorities include parts of Italy, Romania & even Moldova in their definition of the Balkans. I will however leave my journeys in those parts for future publications.

Incidentally, the word 'Balkan' comes from Turkish, meaning mountain, and has been applied to the area since the early 19th century.

Lands of Disharmony

The Balkans instinctively conjure up distasteful images of conflict, disputed territories and ethnic cleansing.

History has indeed shown us time and time again that these are volatile lands with events here having global consequences on a par with those unsolvable differences in the Middle East.

I am a firm believer that if you are visiting foreign lands, you should aim to understand the history of those lands. Only then can you truly appreciate what you experience.

I will cover more of the history in the ensuing chapters, but I will also try to give you a potted history now of events over the past few hundred years.

Empiric Rule (from the mid-14th Century)

Much of the Balkan region formed a major part of the Ottoman Empire over various periods from the mid-14th Century up until the early 20th, with various nationalistic rebellions and uprisings in the main put down.

During the same period that the rest of the Balkans had been under Ottoman occupation, Croatia & Slovenia had formed part of the Habsburg and then the succeeding Austria-Hungary Empires.

In 1822 however, matters started to change as Greece won its independence from the Ottomans.

This was followed around half a century later by the Russo-Turkish War (1877-1878), which led to Russia's allies Serbia, Bulgaria & Montenegro, gaining independence from the ashes of a crushing Ottoman defeat.

Bosnia & Herzegovina fell under Austria-Hungarian rule around this time as that empire also took advantage of the weakened Ottoman position.

18th Century Balkan Peninsular

The Balkan Wars (1912-13)

The first Balkan War started in October 1912 and ended in May 1913, seeing the Balkan League states of Bulgaria, Greece and Serbia & Montenegro defeat the Ottoman Empire and seize large swathes of territory as a result. The war also led to the formation of an independent Albania.

Despite its success, Bulgaria was dissatisfied over the division of the spoils in Macedonia, which provoked the start of the Second Balkan War in June 1913.

Bulgaria attacked its former allies, Serbia and Greece. Serbian and Greek armies repulsed the Bulgarian offensive and counter-attacked, entering Bulgaria.

With Bulgaria also having previously engaged in territorial disputes with Romania, the war also provoked Romanian intervention against Bulgaria.

Additionally, the Ottomans also took advantage of the situation to regain some of their lost territories from the previous war.

When Romanian troops approached the capital Sofia, Bulgaria asked for an armistice, resulting in the Treaty of Bucharest in which Bulgaria had to cede portions of its First Balkan War gains to Serbia, Greece and Romania. In the Treaty of Constantinople, it also lost Edirne to the Ottomans.

The war was over in a little over a month, but the consequences were far reaching.

The Balkan Map in 1878 & After the Balkan Wars

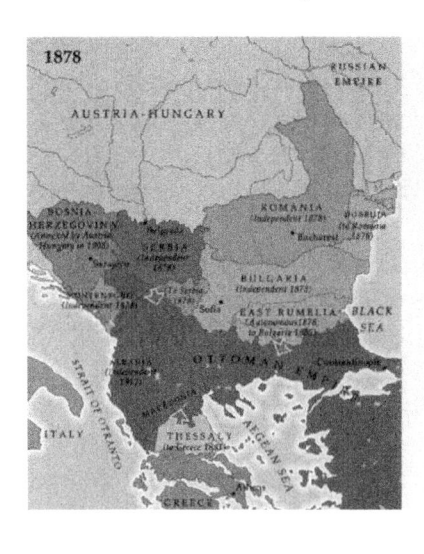

Stay with me!

World Wars

The Balkans was also where World War I emanated from, due to the fallout from the Balkan Wars finally leading to Archduke Franz Ferdinand of Austria-Hungary's assassination in Sarajevo.

The Archduke had been sent by Austria-Hungary as a diplomat to try and quell Bosnian unrest by promoting the idea of the southern Slavs playing a greater role in the empire as a bulwark against Serbian expansionism.

Consequently, after the assassination various treaties were invoked to set the wheels in motion for the Great War.

The war's prime protagonists at its outset were Germany, Austria-Hungary, the Ottoman Empire & Bulgaria, who fought against the UK, France & Russia.

Many other nations were sucked into the fighting, with the Ottomans also taking the opportunity to ethnically cleanse their lands with genocides, most notably against Armenians & Greeks.

These events, together with the Greece seizing territory in East Thrace and Western Anatolia at the end of WWI, led to the Greco-Turkish War (1919-22).

The war ultimately ended with the Greek forces being repelled, Greece giving up those territories it had seized, plus there being a population exchange of around 1.6 million people between Turkey & Greece.

This particular war ended with the Great Fire of Smyrna (modern-day Izmir), which completely destroyed the Greek & Armenian quarters of the city, whilst leaving the Muslim & Jewish quarters undamaged.

The fire raged for nine-days, creating tens of thousands of Greek & Armenian refugees, many of whom were cruelly raped and murdered or forcibly deported to Anatolia, where many perished in extremely harsh conditions.

There are differing accounts of how the fire started and facts regarding the atrocities committed by the Turks are disputed. Whatever the truth may be, this was a human catastrophe of catastrophic proportions.

Following the end of WWI, the new Balkan order was also created with the formation of Yugoslavia under Peter I of Serbia (initially the nation was actually called The Kingdom of Serbs, Croats and Slovenes, but in 1929 King Alexander I changed the name of the state to Yugoslavia, meaning land of the southern Slavs).

After many territorial losses and much in-fighting, the Ottoman Empire formally collapsed in 1922 with the subsequent declaration of the secular Turkish Republic led by Ataturk.

The formal abolition of the Ottoman Sultanate was performed by Grand National Assembly of Turkey on 1 November 1922. The Sultan was declared persona non grata from the lands that the Ottoman Dynasty had ruled since 1299.

The Sultan's expulsion from Turkey was an act that many Muslims still take as a huge insult to the Islamic Faith and is something that jihadis have been trying to avenge ever since.

World War II brought fresh turmoil to the region. As German troops invaded Yugoslavia in 1941, they were welcomed by Croatian fascists. Hitler rewarded the Croats with a nominally independent puppet state, which also incorporated Bosnia.

In the course of a series of overlapping civil wars, widespread atrocities were committed by all sides. In Croatia, Serbs, Jews, gypsies and anti-fascist Croats were killed in concentration camps.

Serbia came under the control of German troops while the Italians occupied Montenegro.

Rival partisans under Josip Broz Tito, a communist, and Dragoljub Mihailovic, a Serb nationalist, fought the Germans, when not fighting each other. Kosovo was occupied by Albanian and Italian troops, whilst the Bulgarians invaded Macedonia.

In 1945 following the end of WWII, Socialist Yugoslavia was declared by Marshall Tito.

The communists were able to deal with national aspirations by creating a federation of six nominally equal republics in Croatia, Montenegro, Serbia, Slovenia, Bosnia-Herzegovina, and Macedonia. The Federal Socialist Republic of Yugoslavia had been born.

In Serbia the two provinces of Kosovo and Vojvodina were given autonomous status, whilst Bulgaria became a communist state at the same time.

The Balkans in 1945

In Yugoslavia, national and ethnic tensions grew over the ensuing post-war decades and when Tito died in 1980 many expected the federation to break up. However, the Slavic nation was to survive uneasily for over a further decade.

It was only a matter of time though for those fundamental differences to boil over into full-scale conflict.

The War in Yugoslavia

The '90s Yugoslav War with its brutality and deep racial hatred was extensively played out on our TV screens in the West. As a result, wonderful cities such as Sarajevo, Dubrovnik, Mostar, Srebrenica & Pristina became synonymous with terror and suffering.

I remember the war being really confusing, with it difficult to make out who was fighting who at any particular stage.

Slovenia and then Croatia were the first to break away from Yugoslavia in 1991, but only at the cost of bloody Croatian conflict with Serbia.

The war in Croatia led to hundreds of thousands of refugees and re-awakened memories of the brutality of the 1940s. By late 1992, a further conflict had broken out in Bosnia, which had also declared independence.

The Serbs who lived there were determined to remain within Yugoslavia and to help build a greater Serbia. They received strong backing from extremist groups in Belgrade.

Bosnian Muslims were driven from their homes in carefully planned operations, many being raped before being brutally murdered and buried in mass graves.

By 1993 the Bosnian Muslim government was besieged in the capital Sarajevo, surrounded by Bosnian Serb forces who controlled around 70% of Bosnia. The deadly siege was to last an incredible 1,425 days.

In Central Bosnia, the mainly Muslim army was fighting a separate war against Bosnian Croats who wished to be part of a greater Croatia. The presence of UN peacekeepers to contain the situation proved totally ineffective.

Long overdue American pressure to end the war eventually led to the Dayton agreement of November 1995, which created two self-governing entities within Bosnia - the Bosnian Serb Republic and the Muslim (Bosnjak)-Croat Federation.

A NATO led peacekeeping force was charged with implementing the military aspects of the peace agreement, primarily overseeing the separation of forces.

Croatia, meanwhile, took back most of the territory earlier captured by Serbs when it waged lightning military campaigns in 1995, which also resulted in the mass exodus of around 200,000 Serbs from Croatia.

In 1998, nine years after the abolition of Kosovo's prior autonomy, the Kosovo Liberation Army, supported by the majority ethnic Albanians, came out in open rebellion against Serbian rule.

The international community, while supporting greater autonomy, opposed the Kosovar Albanians' demand for independence.

However, international pressure grew on Serbian strongman Slobodan Milosevic to bring an end to the escalating violence in the province.

Threats of military action by the West over the continuing crisis culminated in the launching of NATO air strikes against Yugoslavia forces stationed in Kosovo in March 1999, the first attack on a sovereign European country in the NATO alliance's history.

The bombings continued until an agreement was reached that led to the withdrawal of Yugoslav armed forces from Kosovo, and the establishment of a UN peacekeeping mission in Kosovo.

This ultimately brought about the end of the war, with only Serbia (still officially including Kosovo) and Montenegro remaining allied as the remnants of the Yugoslav Republic. This finally ended with Montenegrin independence in 2006, followed by Kosovo in 2008.

21st Century Balkan Peninsular

Summary of Key Dates

13th to 19th Century	The Ottoman Empire rules the majority of the Balkans
16th Century – 1918	The Habsburg Empire and then the succeeding Austria Hungary Empire rules over Slovenia & Croatia
1822	Greece becomes independent after defeating the Ottomans
1877-78	The Russo-Turkey War sees Serbia, Bulgaria & Montenegro gain independence
1878	Rule of Bosnia & Herzegovina passes from the Ottomans to Austria-Hungary
Oct 1912-May 1913	First Balkan War. Greece, Bulgaria and Serbia & Montenegro win territory from the Ottomans. Independent Albania is formed.
June - Aug 1913	Second Balkan War. Greece and Serbia & Montenegro gain territory from Bulgaria, as does Romania
July 1914	World War I breaks out following assassination of Archduke Ferdinand in Sarajevo. Germany, Austria-Hungary, The Ottoman Empire & Bulgaria are at war with the UK, France & Russia
November 1918	World War I ends in defeat for the Ottomans & Austria-Hungary. The Kingdom of Serbs, Croats & Slovenes is formed
1914-22	Mass genocides are perpetrated by the Ottomans against Orthodox Greeks living in modern day Turkey. Reportedly over 1

	million Armenians are murdered at the hands of the Ottoman Turks on what has become known as the Armenian Genocide and still causes a huge rift between the nations
1919-1922	The Greco-Turkish War is fought over territory. Greece agrees to return to pre-WWI borders giving up lands won during the first Balkan War
1922	The Ottoman Empire collapses to be replaced by secular Republic of Turkey
1923	Repatriation of over 1.2 million Orthodox Christians from Turkey to Greece, with 355k Muslims in Greece moving the other way
1929	The Kingdom of Serbs, Croats & Slovenes renamed Yugoslavia, encompassing Serbia (including Kosovo), Croatia, Bosnia & Herzegovina, Macedonia, Montenegro & Slovenia
September 1939	World War II commences
1941	Germany occupies Serbia and Italy do likewise in Montenegro. Fascist Croatia (incorporating Bosnia) gains autonomy. Serbs & Jews are amongst those murdered by Croat regime
May 1945	World War II ends in Europe with Yugoslavia becoming a socialist republic under Marshall Tito and Bulgaria becomes a communist state
1980	Marshall Tito dies, nationalism escalates in Yugoslavia

1991	Slovenia and Croatia declare independence sparking conflict with Serbia. Bosnia & Herzegovina follows suit in 1992
1992-96	Siege of Sarajevo, with Serb forces surrounding the Bosnian capital for 1,425 days
1999	NATO bombing in Yugoslavia ultimately brings the war to an end. Serbia & Montenegro are the only remaining Slavic alliance
2006 & 2008	Montenegro declares independence in May 2006, followed by Kosovo in February 2008

Nowadays

Today tensions still never seem far from the surface in the whole Balkan region. Understandably so when you read what has gone on throughout history. The map would look hugely different if all supposedly valid territorial claims were settled in favour of the claimants.

Whole regions could disappear with their accepted histories rewritten, coastal countries might become landlocked, masses of population could be forced to migrate once more, and great cities may change their names entirely in the same way as Byzantium became Constantinople and then Istanbul.

All of this has happened before and who is to say that history will not repeat itself? After all, we are not exactly blessed with being able to learn the lessons of the past.

For now, the region is an intoxicating and fascinating place to visit. It should definitely be on your travel bucket list if it is not already.

Chapter One – A Short Balkan Interlude
(September 1987)

My first steps inside the Balkans were actually in 1987, for what was to be an extremely brief visit.

I was on my first ever inter-rail trip with a school friend named Poll. We had travelled on a very tight budget and were completely unprepared having just a Thomas Cook European Railway Timetable (forever fondly known as TC in these quarters), the Youth Hostelling in Europe guidebook and a smattering of geographical knowledge.

Things started to go pear-shaped when Poll lost his passport during a drinking spree in Munich.

This meant a trip to the British Embassy in the hope that he may be issued with an emergency replacement. Our wishes were kind of granted, but in truth the document eventually issued was just an official paper designed to enable us to travel back to the UK.

However, we were less than a week into our trip, so pressed on eastwards through Austria. The paper was scrutinised closely at the border control in these pre-Schengen days, but thankfully passed inspection.

We had planned to visit Hungary, securing visas to enable us to head behind the Iron Curtain that still existed in those days. This was now of course not possible due to Poll's visa being neatly stamped in his old mislaid passport.

Yugoslavia was however visa-free, so we still planned to visit Eastern Europe, with Pula, Ljubljana and Dubrovnik all on the list of desired destinations.

TC displayed the route - across the Austrian border into Maribor (now part of Slovenia) and then on to Ljubljana, before heading to the Adriatic Coast the next day.

Guard Against Complacency

The border guards entered the train at Spielfieldstraß, the archetypal scruffy little border station just inside Austria. As the guards approached, our hearts were beating hard. Would Poll's documentation pass?

It was pretty much a paper form, a mug shot of Poll plus a few ink stamps, all accompanied by the signature of the British consular in Munich.

The guards were in our carriage now and just as they reached us the train started to move. At least they could not throw us off in Austria now. Once we were in Yugoslavia, perhaps they would let us continue.

There were four guards in total, all four being six-feet plus with dark unshaven complexion, thick set and stern expressions. One of them was female, perhaps she would take pity on two hapless travellers?

Well, I was no translator of Serbo-Croatian, but by the look on the guards faces and the fact that they passed the 'passport' between themselves whilst shaking their heads, was a sure sign that all was not well.

"You must get off next station and see chief. This not good papers. He decide what to do."

They all carried firearms and to two young travel virgins they were extremely intimidating. The fact that the rest of the train seemed to be staring us only added to our discomfort. We felt like criminals for sure.

We shortly arrived in Maribor train station, another shabby affair.

There was no sign of the guards though. Perhaps they had let us get away with it after all?

"Come with me," boomed the English-speaking border official as he approached where we sat. Bummer, our hopes were dashed.

As our train went off into the distance towards Zagreb, we were led to a small office. All four guards accompanied us into the cramped space where a balding man sat behind a desk. He had a bigger moustache, larger gun and a lot more decoration on his shirt pocket than the others. He was obviously head honcho.

He grabbed Poll's paperwork and studied it in detail for what seemed an age.

The silence was broken with a Slavic discussion that lasted a good five minutes. They seemed to be debating something. Was this a good sign? We soon had an answer to that one.

"Where are you going in Yugoslavia, how long will you stay, how much money do you have?" Clearly only one of these questions was important to them.

The guards did not care that we were going to Pula and may stay for three or four days. They did however care that we only had a few dinar & twenty pounds sterling in readies and had zero interest in the fact that we had some Eurocheques, with a credit card for emergencies only.

With no cash to speak of to bribe our way in, our fate was sealed. In any case, our connecting train to Ljubljana had also just left the station.

More Slavic debate followed by stilted English. "You cannot continue Yugoslavia. You return Austria with guard. Train go fifteen minutes."

There was no more debate. We didn't even try to argue, as we were savvy enough to know that this would be futile without at least £100 (about £300 in today's money) in ready money to buy our way in.

I just had time to spend the dinar note that I had managed to garner in the UK at the station kiosk to buy two beers and a packet of crackers. Some small crumbs of comfort at least.

Then our transport back to the West arrived. A huge snake of a freight train with what can best be described as a wooden cattle car attached behind the locomotive, in turn connected to countless container carriages that stretched further than the eye could see in the dimming light.

We were beckoned aboard the cattle car (a good four-foot climb) to join the four guards for the journey back over the border.

Seating was a choice between sacks of grain or the wooden floor. A weak light came on once the loco fired up again and we were on our way.

We made out our musty smelling surroundings in the dimly lit wagon. Grain strewn across the floor, empty sacks piled up to the ceiling, gaps in the floorboards revealing the tracks below, a small pile of broken glass, dozens of dead flies and equal number of living gnats, together with the odd fluttering moth head-butting the bare light bulb.

It was the sort of place where they torture people in films – dark, dank and away from civilisation. I was just pleased to see that there was no wooden chair and rope lying around!

As the guards drank vodka and played cards, we consumed our beer & crackers and discussed our experience whilst sat on lumpy sacks. We agreed that we would laugh about it one day. Not yet though in case this could be misconstrued by the guards as contempt or something else that may lead to more hassle.

Poll spent the rest of the journey drooling over the chiseled features of the female guard, whilst I flicked through TC and batted away midges. TC's small print was hard to read in the night-light. I thought I made out that the next train out of Spielfieldstraß was six next morning, some eight hours away. We really hoped that I had misread.

After twenty-five minutes we had arrived back in the tiny Austrian station, our final destination. The guards marched off into the darkness, deep in conversation and seemingly now oblivious to our presence. We watched them leave through the light of their torches until we could see or hear them no more.

We conjectured whether they were off for a naughty vodka fueled card game. I had to stop Poll from going after them on the strength of that vision!

Once the train also left in the same direction as the guards to deliver its freight somewhere, all was quiet. We really were in the middle of nowhere it seemed. There was nothing but the train tracks, a small station building, some shadowy trees and our bemused selves standing in the dark.

The backdoor to the station was locked - oh no, you don't say, surely not!

Thankfully the front door was open - we turned on the light to reveal two benches a timetable and a closed ticket window.

The timetable confirmed our fears, eight hours until the first train out of there, heading to Graz. We then eyed the benches again, imagining them as our beds for the night.

Poll had noticed some lights up the hill, so we headed that way hoping to find a bar open. After a ten-minute struggle up the steep incline with our rucksacks seemingly gaining in weight, we reached our goal. There was indeed a bar, right in the middle of a number of houses. Hallelujah!

In fact, the bar was a converted house and the drinking area was clearly once a lounge. We gratefully ordered a beer & pickled egg each and slumped onto the sofa.

It was nice and warm, so we hoped that it was one of those 'stay open until the last man leaves' type bars you get on the continent. The sofa was infinitely preferable to the station benches after all.

Sadly, our hopes were soon dashed as the surly bar lady tersely informed us that we had to drink up and leave. She resembled an East German discus thrower from the '70s and was clearly not open to negotiation, let alone a sneaky after-hours half.

We played it out for as long as we could whilst the owner tapped her fingers on the bar tutting loudly. We had outstayed our 'welcome' by some stretch, soon having no choice but to load ourselves back up once more to head downhill to our 'accommodation'.

A Bum Note

It was now raining, but thankfully it didn't take long to get into the dry once more, the heavy rucksacks giving us forward momentum down the hill.

Despite being inside it was still cold and we were a little damp, so we clambered almost fully dressed into our sleeping bags. Poll placed an empty drinks can against the door, supposedly to act as an alarm if anybody else should have the temerity to enter OUR bedroom.

This makeshift alarm was sadly not required as only a couple of moments later we heard voices that grew louder as they approached.

Even though they were Germanic voices, we could tell that they were the slurred voices of drunks and by the sounds of it there were at least three of them.

The first grubby bearded tramp peered through the window and was soon joined by his three almost identical mates.

The pair of us were clearly on their manor; uninvited guests who would not, as it happened, spoil their party. Poll and I looked at each other. Blast, there goes any notion of sleep!

The tramp troupe entered the dry fray each clutching a bottle of schnapps. The stink was almost unbearable, making both of us instantly nauseous and regretting having a second pickled egg!

The obnoxious quartet chose to totally ignore us, lost in their own inebriated world. A noisy, dirty, smelly, drunken world.

We could no longer chance sleep for fear of being robbed blind or worse. Poll stood to his full six-foot plus frame, as if to show he was not to be messed with.

Hurriedly we hatched a plan for a one-hour watch followed by a one-hour kip in rotation. The plan was fatally flawed due to A) a rock-hard bench not long enough to take a whole body & B) the stink and noise coming from the vagrants.

It was gone four by the time the last of the bums fell into a snoring drunken stupor and by that time we were both wide awake, all chance of sleep long since gone.

Instead we viewed the snoring heap of failure before us. As if in uniform, they all had filthy thick grey overcoats, sturdy but well-worn steel-capped black boots, stained jeans, ripped V-neck jumpers, worn out shirts and thick black beards.

We could only wonder what their underwear was like, a thought that was hard to dispel with the smells and involuntary noises emanating from their sweating bodies. Disgusting.

The whole place would probably need fumigating; we surmised that the station staff would need to use a whole aerosol can of air freshener spray at least!

Eventually after three excruciatingly boring & uncomfortable hours and despite there still being over an hour until the train was due, we decided to venture outside, the sub-zero cold being preferable to gas poisoning. At least it had stopped raining.

We soon had the entertainment of the station staff arriving to kick out the unwelcome visitors. This was clearly a daily ritual.

Each slumbering tramp was prodded with a rod and enticed to stand with the offer of a bread roll, before after ten-minutes of waking up grunts and stretches, the tramps staggered out once more into their daily routine whilst devouring their morning sustenance.

Cue mop, water and the predicted air freshener!

I asked one station-worker why they did not lock at night and he explained that cleaning products were cheaper than repairing broken glass and doorframes!

The sight of the early morning train to Graz was one of the most welcome sights I have ever seen. Right on time our escape arrived. The wonderful luxury of a heated train, takeaway coffee & croissant and ninety-minutes sleep in a compartment all to ourselves. Bliss!

Not the ideal first Balkan experience. The only way was up after that. Right?

Chapter Two – Byzantine
(October 2006)

The Ancient Eastern Roman Empire became known as the Byzantine Empire. Encompassing much of the Middle East & Balkans, it was the most powerful economic, cultural and military force in Europe during its existence of over one thousand years.

The core of the Empire, which dated back to 330 AD and finally fell to the Ottomans in 1453, centered on modern day Turkey and Greece, with its ancient capital called Byzantium.

In 2006 we decided to traverse a good portion of the former Empire's core by rail.

We had booked our late October flight to Istanbul from where we would take the Toros Express via Ankara, Adana and Antakya to Aleppo in Syria. We had talked about this trip for several years and were determined to do it as soon as possible.

Hamish & I really love the Middle East having had already visited Israel, Palestine, Lebanon & Jordan together, but travel there can be unpredictable with the uneasy peace always liable to break at any time.

This is exactly what happened in 2006. Shortly after we booked our flights, Israel decided it needed to bomb Hezbollah out of neighboring Lebanon. Much of Southern Lebanon was hit including Beirut's airport.

Thousands of Lebanese fled over the border into Syria. It seemed only a matter of time before Syria would be sucked into a war protecting its ally, much of which it actually had occupied from 1976 until the 2005 assassination of former Lebanese Prime Minister Rafic Hariri, an act that Syrian officials were accused of perpetrating.

Mrs Wilbur and Mrs Hamish put their collective feet down meaning our trip on the Toros had to be put on hold. So, what to do with our flight to Istanbul?

Time to dust off the TC then. A rail route taking in Thessaloniki, Skopje, Niš in Serbia and Sofia was sketched out and an early November flight home from the Bulgarian capital purchased. It was time to re-kindle the spirit of inter-rail!

Bazaar Practice

We had both been to Istanbul before, so this would be a short one-night stop before the overnight train into Greece the next day.

Istanbul was the fulcrum of the Byzantine Empire, where East meets West, where Europe ends and Asia starts. It has had an amazingly checkered history with not only name changes, but also different rulers.

The settlement was founded by Thracian tribes between the 13th and 11th centuries BC, when it was known as Lygos. It was colonised by the Greeks in the 7th century BC, before falling to the Roman Empire in AD 196 and being then renamed Byzantium. In 330 it was renamed yet again as Constantinople and made the new capital of the Eastern Roman Empire.

The city rose to be the largest of the western world, with a population peaking at close to half a million people. The Byzantine Empire ended with the Muslim conquest in 1453 with Constantinople then becoming the capital of the Ottoman Empire.

It was shortly after this time that the Greek Orthodox church Hagia Sophia, which had been built around AD 537, was converted into a mosque and renamed Ayasofya. Despite the conversion much of the interior Christian Byzantine decoration remains.

It is also worth mentioning at this stage that during the 16th century golden period of the Ottoman Empire under Suleiman the Magnificent, it controlled most of South Eastern Europe, including present-day Hungary, the Balkan region, Greece, and parts of Ukraine, portions of the Middle East now modern day Iraq, Syria, Israel, Palestine and Egypt, parts of Africa as far west as Algeria and large parts of the Arabian Peninsula.

The Ottomans of course left an indelible mark on the history of Europe, spreading the Islamic religion to several countries, suppressing Christian worship & Western arts at the same time and leading to the barbaric Crusades launched from Western powers.

Wounds from that period run deep, especially in the uneasy relationship between Greece & Turkey. A sense of injustice prevails, accentuated by the enforced population exchange of 1923 when over 1.2 million Greeks left Turkey for Greece and more than 350,000 Turks made the opposite journey.

When the Republic of Turkey was founded in 1923, the capital was moved from Constantinople to Ankara and since 1930 the Turkish name Istanbul has been the sole official name of the city.

I digress, back to 2006.

We agreed that the Grand Bazaar was the place to head, as we had already seen the Blue Mosque, Ayasofya Mosque and the Topkapi Palace on previous visits.

On my first trip there in the late eighties I had been with another ex-schoolmate called Lang. We too had visited the Grand Bazaar and I had to explain the rules of barter to my friend.

"Just bid what you think the item is worth and stick to it. Remember however, if the bargaining reaches agreement, you must conclude the deal or it will become a huge incident."

Lang was soon approached by a man selling a bundle of seven pairs of white socks, for which he wanted £4 worth of Turkish Lire.

Keen to practice his newly learned bartering skills and get some comic effect, Lang waded in with a bid to the value of fifty pence, one eighth of what the trader wanted.

He was met with a toothless grin. "My friend, these are quality socks, I won't take anything less than £3."

With me looking on encouragingly (well laughing quite a lot actually), Lang stuck to his guns, "Fifty pence."

"But feel the quality, they are better than you find in the shops...... oh you really kill me....... OK, £2."

"I will pay fifty pence." Of course, Lang didn't really want the socks but was enjoying the contest. He always was a good bluffer at card games and he was turning into a good barterer too.

Cue the sock seller shaking his head and walking away, only to turn on his heels when we started to do likewise. "I need to feed my family, I am only a poor merchant, you are rich Westerner. OK £1 but only so my family can eat."

This was too much for Lang, who caved in at that price and sealed the deal with a handshake.

Change for £20 worth of lire? No problem, as the 'impoverished' salesman brought out a large wad of notes. So much for poverty!

So, we were now sorted if we wanted a game of tennis, at least in the sock wear department!

In 2006 it was just spice that grabbed our attention, snapping up some Persian saffron and local nutmeg to keep the ladies happy back home. We declined to buy the Arabian Viagra or snake powder aphrodisiac - we had no need of that quite yet to keep our ladies happy!

That evening we sampled some local fare (salad, hummus, beer and shisha pipe), before returning merrily to our Ottoman style five-story hotel for a nightcap courtesy of Ahmad the night porter and his bottle of sickly-sweet brown liquid.

We quipped that Ahmad's huge bushy moustache had consumed more of the liqueur than Ahmad himself!

Next morning, we set off straight after breakfast to the train station. We hadn't been able to reserve our train tickets in England and on visiting Sirkeci Station that morning at ten, we were told to return at three that afternoon when the international desk would be open.

When we returned five hours later, the desk was indeed open. The same desk as we had enquired at earlier and with the same grey-haired gentleman sat behind it.

He now had a tent style card in front of him stating 'international ticket sales' and he wore a blue peaked cap. No comment or query was necessary, just a wry smile and a nod. That was just the way it worked in these parts!

We procured tickets for that nights' overnight sleeper. Gloriously the tickets were hand written in duplicate and the purchase recorded by hand in a huge ledger. A few ink stamps later and £80 worth of lire and the tickets were ours.

The ticket seller twitched his grey cigarette stained moustache and smiled weakly as he handed the paper bundle over and wished us a good journey. Job done, so we could now relax.

Shaken & Stirred

Earlier that day we had passed a hammam called Cağaloğlu Hamami, whose sign proclaimed it as being listed in the book '1,000 things to do before you die'. We decided that it was definitely something to do before we boarded.

So, it was here that we headed with our rucksacks for ablutions & scrubbing to ensure that we would be the cleanest travellers on board the train that evening.

Neither of us had ever experienced this before and only had an idea of what was in store from watching the BBC travel programme 'Around the World in Eighty Days' with Michael Palin. He had survived with no broken bones despite a real pummeling, so we figured it would also be fine.

On entry we were handed a 'treatment' menu. It resembled one that you get in a car wash and we opted for the equivalent of wash, scrub, polish and chamois.

For about £20 worth of lire, we purchased the all-inclusive.

We each had a small wooden booth measuring one metre by one metre to change in. It was like being in an enclosed horse drawn carriage of the type Victorian bathers used to use to enter the bracing English Channel.

Four wooden steps led up to the red-carpeted cubicle. A small wooden chair to sit on, a trio of hooks and a locker for your valuables were the sum of the rest of the parts.

The place was unisex, but during our visit it was men only in situ and many just hung out (literally, as they wore only skimpy towels), drinking tea and playing backgammon.

The Cağaloğlu was built in 1741 by order of Sultan Mahmut I and didn't seem to have changed much since. Marble baths and floors, alabaster columns, over thirty wooden changing cabins on two levels, the upper tier accessed by wooden staircase and fronted by a wooden balcony that stretched the full perimeter of the main hall.

I took my modesty preserving tea towel and threadbare bath towel into my booth and soon exited to meet up with a grinning Hamish for our over-priced hamam experience.

Shuffling and slipping, we made our way to the action areas. We had been given some over-sized flipflops to wear. I personally hate this type of footwear and must have resembled some sort of handicapped seal as it made its way along the beach to the water's edge.

Our ablutions started very gently with a nice warm solo wash in the thermal waters, using the after-eight mint sized bar of soap we had been handed.

Next stop the steam room designed to open your pores and let the vapors purify your body. You soon felt yourself cooking in there, so I figured that thirty-four seconds was plenty long enough. Hamish lasted nineteen!

Third stop was the painful bit, a scrub at the hands of our male bathing attendant. A paid assassin in a nappy. This was what the scrubbing mitt that came with our package was for.

38

The six-foot-four brute then took great pleasure in making us "as clean as when you were baby." I went before Hamish, who sat on the hot stones watching as I was thrown about and soaked.

The scrubbing was excruciating, especially around the nipple area. As I winced in pain, I also chuckled thinking about Hamish having his turn. "Enjoy the spectacle while you can matey!"

The whole experience was pretty uncomfortable to say the least – a bit like a session in a dentist's chair or having a childhood haircut at the hands of an impatient, heavy-handed barber.

After about eight minutes, which seemed considerably longer I can tell you, we were done. The amount of black dead skin that had been removed from my body was incredible. And I thought I was already clean! The mitt was mine to keep, never to be used again though - far too barbaric.

It was now happily Hamish's turn. Predictably he winced (actually more like squealed!) with pain as the beast went to work with his mitt. I killed myself laughing but tried my best to conceal this from the attendants lest they had 'special' treatment still to mete out in the massage finale.

Entertainment over, it was quickly time for the final installment, the massage. Oh shit, here goes! If the scrub was three out of five on the pain scale, the massage averaged about six!

I was thrown, twisted, bent, kneed, slapped and sat on. At the end I felt an absolute million dollars. Bones had creaked and muscles had been beaten into submission, but the effects meant that I was now floating on thin air.

Hamish looked on with a mixture of mirth, bewilderment and horror. It was now his turn. The whole episode was repeated on my buddy who yelped, strained, struggled and gasped through the 'ordeal', much to my amusement once more.

We both agreed it was well worth it. If I am honest, I prefer the genteel touch of a young lady in white uniform over a huge, oily bloke with thick black hair, square jaw, bristling moustache and dressed only in a revealing loin cloth, but the after effects were amazing.

We had also shed many grammes of dead skin and grime and were now probably indeed the purest we had been (on the outside anyway) since baby days!

Gliding back to the main hall, we were rewarded with an apple tea and a few knowing looks from the backgammon players. Another couple of tourists put through their paces and paying handsomely for the privilege!

As I sipped my tea, I wondered how many of the other 999 'must-dos' I had done already and how many more I would do yet...

After changing and grabbing a quick falafel opposite, we returned to Sirkeci station at around 19.30 ready for the 20.00 to Thessaloniki. Just time to buy a few cans of EFES dark and some cheesy potato crisps from the shop outside, before we found our private berths.

Istanbul to Thessaloniki Departure 20.00 Arrival 10.05, 508 KM

This was our first overnight train in Europe since those heady inter-rail days and we were very excited. The compartment may have been cramped as usual but we were going to have a party.

Beer and crisps plus geographical quizzes, the ten must do things before dying etc. etc.

Racket

Our accommodation was spartan as usual – the modern conveniences limited to two metal bunk beds, tiny sink, luggage rack, broken temperature control and a reading light each.

Luckily the temperature was good so we did not need anything other than a climate as nature intended, nor did we require the rather itchy looking grey blankets.

The beds had already been made up with pristine white sheets, so we were just thinking of turning in for the night when what can only be described as a sound of a cat being strangled came from the next-door compartment.

"What the blazes was that?" we both exclaimed, or words to that effect. It was now gone midnight.

The appalling noise continued - was something or someone in distress right next door to us, we wondered?

I had to investigate. My t-shirt was hurriedly stretched on and I headed straight to our train neighbour's door.

The curtains were drawn and the light was out, but as the wailing continued I could just about spy through the small gap to make out the silhouette of a person sat cross-legged on the floor, blowing into a contraption that resembled bagpipes.

Hamish soon joined me along with two other bewildered passengers.

"It's someone playing bagpipes," I informed the perplexed trio.

Hamish understood, but the other two were non-English speaking Turks. I invited them to see for themselves. They soon understood too, the woman of the middle-aged couple being dispatched to find the train guard.

All this time the 'music' continued, still a wailing, tuneless assault on our eardrums.

After about ten minutes the guard returned with the Turkish lady. On hearing the noise, the clearly irritated guard rapped on the door with his master key.

The racket continued unabated, forcing the master key to be used. With the light aggressively switched on, we all peered inside to see the cause of the commotion.

A dark-skinned youth had removed the mattress from his bed and now sat upon it blowing into some tubes that were attached to an inflated sheep's stomach. Even with the door open and the light on he continued to blow, his expressionless eyes fixed into a stare straight above us.

42

It was immediately clear that he was on something hallucinogenic and the guard had a challenge on his hands to shake some sense into him. It took a good two minutes for the youth to realise anybody was there and only then did he stop making the eerie sounds.

At this point he shouted out in Turkish and jolted backwards looking startled and frightened.

The last we saw of him and his meagre possessions was as he disappeared down the corridor with the chuntering guard. He went like a lamb, still in his own little world.

We could only imagine how he would feel when he came to his senses, perhaps ejected in some strange and dark border station or handed over to the transport police for drug possession and disturbing the peace.

Drama over, we returned to our lovely beds and slept soundly, despite the discomfort of the odd stray crisp under the covers.

The early morning border control disturbed our slumber and we thought once more of the young bagpipe player, wondering what had become of him. His compartment remained empty so we figured whatever he had encountered would not have led to a happy ending for him.

Turkish Railways rule 15, subsection 15.5, clause XIII – 'travellers must refrain from playing all wind instruments after dark. Penalty is to have said instrument inserted somewhere unpleasant!'

At around seven, the bedding was collected at the border station and our bedroom converted to a normal carriage. Some old Greek women going home to their villages soon joined us.

We pulled in at our destination around ten in the morning, some two hours late. We were to find that a late arrival would be a fairly typical experience.

We had averaged less than forty KMH with all the border controls and a locomotive change en-route. Having spent much of the journey asleep it did not matter a jot.

The thrill of a night train is often at the expense of a magical viewing gallery from your seat that you may get with daytime journeys, especially during winter when daylight hours are condensed.

I therefore have no idea of the terrain we had traversed, or whether I would have seen waving kids and field-workers, nor had I had a decent chance to interact with fellow passengers.

Still, I had been more than content with this particular journey that joined neighbouring nations with an uneasy relationship. Sadly, as I write this route no longer exists, but will hopefully be reinstated at some stage.

Thessaloniki is the capital of the Greek region of Macedonia (more on that particular name to come) and Greece's second largest city. Unusually however it is only the third most populous Greek speaking city, ranking behind Melbourne in Australia.

The word diaspora comes from an ancient Greek word meaning 'to scatter about' and is the word used to describe people who migrate away from their homeland. Greeks have certainly scattered over the years to escape conflict, political turmoil and economic hardship.

There are large Greek populations not only in Australia, but also Canada, United States, Germany and latterly in the UK and other European countries, following the most recent financial crisis.

We decided to save a few Euros and walk to our hotel, it also always being a good idea to do a few yomps straining under the weight of your backpack to get that authentic inter-rail feel!

I immediately felt at home. My wife is Athenian and I had a decent grasp of the language. I remembered how weird the Greek writing looked on my first visit in '94, but now I could read pretty well, compared to the average traveller anyhow.

We smiled at the amusingly named Hotel Vergina as we passed, until after twenty-five minutes brisk walking we arrived at our clean and smart hotel near the waterfront.

'Kalimera. Ehoume ena vomatio yia mia nikta.'

I felt good that I was able to say we had a room for the night. My grammar and accent were awful, but I impressed Hamish and was just about understood by the receptionist, who humored me by stating how impressed she was with my attempt at Greek.

Empty Vessels

We were meeting my wife's nieces and cousins that evening for a meal. Joanna was studying topography in Thessaloniki whilst her sister Mary and parents Rania and George were paying her a visit from their home near Korinthos.

We had plenty of time to explore, walking the length of the promenade up to the famous White Tower and statue of Alexander the Great.

The sea was calm, a couple of tankers were anchored at the horizon, a military ship moved slowly away into the distance and a couple of deserted pleasure boats were moored by the harbour wall, ready for pulsating music and social drinking later that evening.

The water was really clear at the shoreside and large blue jellyfish were evident in large numbers, swaying back and forth in the gentle current.

The promenade was lined with cafés and bars and plenty of guys and girls had set up camp to see and be seen. We did likewise and did plenty of seeing, mainly groups of attractive student girls and their beaus.

Thessaloniki is a big student town and they clearly did not have many lectures that day by the looks of the numbers that strolled or drank frappe. It was a nice and sunny October day, perfect for leisurely pursuits like people watching.

We met my wife's relatives at the hotel that evening. Lots of hugs and kisses - well I hadn't seen Hamish for a few minutes! Seriously the Greeks love to hug and kiss and Hamish was welcomed as a lifelong friend.

This despite never having properly met before, even though Hamish had been best man at my 'Big Fat Greek Wedding' in Athens, which the others naturally attended too.

Like my wife, cousin Rania was named after their mutual paternal grandmother, as is the way in Hellenic families. She worked as a hospital administrator in Korinthos whilst George had his own topography business in their hometown of Kyato, hence Joanna's choice of study.

Only the previous year, 'cousin' Rania had taken me to one of my bucket list must see sites – the incredible Corinth Canal.

The 6.4-kilometre-long, 21.4-metre-wide man-made canal separates the Gulf of Corinth and the Aegean, effectively separating the Peloponnese from the Greek mainland.

We had a lovely meal at a local taverna. Everybody spoke good English, so that was how conversation was conducted. The drinks flowed; the food was great and the conversation better.

I even practiced some more of my basic Greek to order the food and remarkably we got exactly what we wanted.

I only blotted my linguistic copybook when asking for the bill. "To loyyarismo parakalo" (the bill please), which has always been an unfathomable tongue twister for me!

We bade a fond farewell around 23.30 and decided to head for the waterfront for a night watch, I mean nightcap!

Hamish settled for a 9% Chimay Brun - obviously not planning an early start then! My choice was McFarland red beer, a tipple that I drank throughout the Athens Olympics in 2004 and now loved. It is amazingly good for a beer brewed by Heineken.

Non-Parade

Next day was a special day. Known as 'Ochi Day', the 28th October commemorates the time that Greece's dictatorial and royalist Prime Minister Metaxas said an emphatic 'NO' in response to an ultimatum made by Italian dictator Mussolini on 28th October 1940.

The ultimatum had been to allow Italian troops and their allies to occupy strategically important parts of Greece.

The Greek refusal led to an immediate Italian invasion from Albania and Greece being pulled into WWII. In April 1941 Germany also invaded, by which time Metaxas was already dead from natural causes.

Despite the hardships that the war brought about, the refusal to accede to Italy's demands was popular with most of the Greek population at the time and has been celebrated every year since with military and student parades.

Slightly worse for wear, we joined the local crowds on the streets to see marching bands along with a show of Greece's military arsenal of tanks, missiles, jets and assorted armoured vehicles.

It was an impressive sight, no doubt sending a message to Greece's near neighbours/foes at the same time.

Later that day we took a train south to Meteora, famed for its mountain top monasteries and convents.

🚂 Thessaloniki to Kalabaka via Larissa, Departure 16.17 Arrival 19.25, 235 KM

The train left on time. Just as well as we only had a seven-minute gap between arriving at Larissa and boarding another train to the town of Kalabaka, base point for Meteora.

All thankfully went smoothly, with us arriving in Larissa just under one and three-quarter hours since we departed, our connecting train happily already in situ waiting for us.

On the Rocks

We arrived early evening and checked into our small hotel for a single night. Stelios and his wife Kiria (Greek for Mrs) Maria owned the comfortable log cabin style lodgings.

Stelios was far from your stereotypical rural Greek hotel owner.

In his seventies and with a full head of grey hair, he still looked fit as a flea in his lumberjack shirt (opened far enough to reveal his grey chest rug) and sturdy walking boots.

He offered to take us on a fifty kilometre hike next day to take in all the sites for €25 each. We politely declined but were in no doubt that his offer had been genuine and was a trek that he did frequently with guests decidedly fitter/more easily persuaded than us.

In an attempt to change our minds, he advised that if the walk was easy enough to be undertaken by a seventy-eight-year-old man, then it would be simple for a couple of young men like us.

What he failed to mention was that he was born and bred in the area and had been doing the journeys regularly since he was a small boy.

In contrast Kiria Maria was short and dumpy and had the tell-tale smell of an ouzo drinker. Dressed top to toe in black in memory of her sister who had died ten months previously, she did epitomise the stereotype of a Greek yaya (grandmother).

We somehow doubted that she did much trekking, but she clearly wore the trousers in this household. It was her that took our room fees and she seemed to lambast poor Stelios for failing to persuade us to hire his guide services.

In Greece there is a saying that the man is the head of the family but the mother is the neck, turning the head in the direction that she wants. Maria was a definite neck (and pain in his) all right.

Our room was uncluttered but comfortable with two wooden beds stood atop stripped wooden floorboards, flanked by wood walls and ceiling with its wooden fan.

The fresh smell of natural pinewood permeated the living & sleeping area, whilst the manufactured aroma of pine cleaner dominated the white tiled bathroom.

The curtains were two Greek flags, lest we wake up and believe that we were in the Swiss Alps by mistake. Maria and Stelios were clearly patriots.

We just had time to get our bearings before darkness fell. We would take it easy that night as next day we would be doing some serious walking on top of the huge rock formations that gave Meteora its name (from Greek it translates as 'suspended rocks').

We ate a vegetarian pizza and watched a Greek football match on TV afterwards (the fact that fading Brazilian superstar Rivaldo was playing for Olympiakos, is all I remember of the game) before an early night.

Inconvenient Convents

Next morning it was one of those priceless moments when you have to be there to fully appreciate it. Breakfast was a DIY affair in a communal kitchen at one end of the hotel. We shared the kitchen/diner with a German couple and their two young sons, who were all dressed up like mountaineers.

Hamish decided that he wanted muesli to fuel his hike and there was a brand-new packet there, waiting for us fresh in its sealed inner packaging.

Hamish tugged at the top of the packaging as instructed but started to get quite a sweat on as the contents refused to reveal themselves. He decided that more force was required; the problem was that when he only needed to ramp up the effort a notch or two, he went straight into 'all his might mode'.

Predictably the packet exploded and its contents were vaulted all around the kitchen, sprinkling the bemused Germans in nuts, oats and berries. For a second or two it was raining Alpen!

"Mein Gott," exclaimed the alarmed frau, before we all broke into fits of laughter as we dusted ourselves down. We were soon tucking into crusty bread and Laughing Cow, whilst leaving Hamish to get to work with the dustpan and brush!

I should imagine that the owners thought their latest guests had a huge appetite, the only way to explain a whole new packet of muesli being consumed.

Maybe the odd hazelnut being found in unexpected places would give them a clue to what really happened at some stage. Either that or Hamish's bright red ears would give the game way, always a clear signal that he was flustered about something.

Luckily, we did not need to explain to Maria who was still comatose from her ouzo-induced sleep, so left undisturbed by the kitchen commotion. Stelios had long since left for a hike alone, no doubt aiming to get some peace.

After breakfast, we took one look at the steep ascent before us and unanimously agreed - taxi up, walk down.

Our time spent on top of the rocks was magic. The monks and nuns lived perched high up on the top of rock formations. The constructions were major feats of building and had stood for several centuries.

Originally built to be inaccessible to the outside world and especially the occupying Turks, the Greek Orthodox monasteries and convents are now big tourist attractions.

Each had pulleys that had enabled supplies to be winched up from below. Originally this was the only way up for the inhabitants as well as goods!

They must have been pretty treacherous places to get to in winter, a world away from normal civilization and definitely not exactly welcoming to uninvited guests.

That day we visited all six sanctuaries, walking several miles and many steep steps in the process. Not quite fifty kilometres maybe but tiring all the same in the hotter than usual winter air.

One of the monasteries eerily displayed the skull of every monk who had lived and died there - at least they had stopped short of preserving their brains in formaldehyde to retain all that pious wisdom!

I bought a small icon to remember the place by and a few blessed 'church things' (minute pillows of multi-coloured fabrics that had been blessed by the monks) to ward off any evil spirits that may be lurking.

We kept our promise and walked down, initially over stone pathways and latterly through a forest. As we neared the bottom, we passed herds of black and brown mountain goats perched precariously on boulders. "Feed the Goat and he will score," I sang in celebration of Manchester City's cult ex-striker Shaun Goater, known affectionately to all City fans as the Goat.

After a quick bite, we caught the late afternoon train back to Thessaloniki, again with a change at Larissa.

When we made the change, it was pitch black and signage was poor. There were two trains due at the same time - one going north which we wanted and the other south to Athens. By hook or by crook we got on the right one and arrived back at our hotel at nine to be reunited with our rucksacks (an arrangement I had made unsurprisingly in English).

There was just time for a takeaway pizza, washed down with Chimay/McFarland on the waterfront, before bed.

Next day we had an early start to catch the train to the Former Yugoslav Republic of Macedonia (FYROM). My feet were sore from the previous day's exerts and so I decided to ceremoniously discard my ill-fitting walking boots, leaving them arranged neatly sticking out of the small waste paper bin.

I supposed they would give the chambermaid a chuckle, or even be turned into an unusual planter.

Chapter Three – A Tale of Three Cities

Thessaloniki – Skopje Departure 7.44 Arrival 11.25, 199KM

We dragged ourselves to the train station after an earlier than desirable alarm call & rapid breakfast. Our giant locomotive was readying itself for the off when we clambered aboard the spartan and well-worn carriage.

We had already purchased our tickets when we had left two days prior to go to Meteora. It is always best to avoid any potential mishaps on the morning of departure if possible.

As it happened the ticket office was open and even though ours was the only train scheduled to go in the following three hours, the queue was already large/intolerable. A good move then to have had some foresight.

I have experienced a fair few Greek queues down the years – definitely not a place for the meek or fainthearted!

What's in a Name?

The Macedonian name is a very touchy subject in Greece. If you look at the maps of the Balkan Region through the ages you will work out why, with historically the whole of Macedonia being part of Greece.

The regions of Greece as they have been since World War II

Nowadays, the 'old' Macedonia is divided into the Greek region of the same name (of which Thessaloniki is the regional capital as I mentioned), which borders the nation that also lays claim to the Macedonian name and heritage.

The Greeks have long objected to FYROM calling itself Macedonia, fearing they would later lay claim to the bordering Greek territories.

Bulgaria, Turkey and Albania would also like a little slice of Greece for themselves, just to add to the regional tensions. Be careful to never mention former US Secretary of State Henry Kissinger (himself a Jewish refugee who fled Nazi Germany) in Greek circles, as he once controversially stated that the Balkan region would be a far more peaceful place if Greece did not exist!

This is what he is reported as saying in 1974 to a group of businessmen in Washington DC, *"The Greek people are anarchic and difficult to tame. For this reason, we must strike deep into their cultural roots: Perhaps then we can force them to conform.*

I mean, of course, to strike at their language, their religion, their cultural and historical reserves, so that we can neutralize their ability to develop, to distinguish themselves, or to prevail; thereby removing them as an obstacle to our strategically vital plans in the Balkans, the Mediterranean, and the Middle East."

For Kissinger's actions in negotiating a ceasefire in Vietnam, he received the 1973 Nobel Peace Prize. The Greek nation would happily have stripped him of it in 1974!

Just to stir up patriotic feelings even more, FYROM claimed ethnic Greek Macedonian military genius and empire builder Alexander the Great as one of their own, mischievously naming Skopje's Airport and main highway after him, plus also erecting countless statues in his honour.

Alexander was of course well-known for spreading the Greek language, religion and culture, not its Slavic equivalents.

The name row has continuously rumbled since the Slavic Macedonia's 1991's independence declaration that followed the break-up of the Yugoslav Republic.

Greece has up until now vetoed any notion of FYROM becoming a member of both the EU and NATO, whilst there has been much impasse and recrimination, despite some of the world's most capable politicians trying to broker a compromise agreement.

As recently as 2018 there seemed that there may have been a breakthrough, as the new government in Skopje and their Greek counter-parts agreed a deal in principle.

As a result, FYROM dropped the Alexander the Great moniker from its airport and main highway due to the Greek government agreeing in principle to FYROM being officially called the Republic of North Macedonia and then being welcomed into the EU & NATO.

A referendum was held in the Republic of Macedonia in September 2018, with voters overwhelmingly affirming support for EU and NATO membership by accepting the agreement, albeit with only a 37% voter turnout – well below the 50 per cent required for the ballot to be legally valid.

There is now commonly accepted suspicion of Russian interference in making the vote constitutionally non-binding through social media manipulation and spreading of rhetoric designed to whip up nationalistic fervor.

Of course, Russia does not particularly want any more NATO or EU foes. Conspiracy theory or fact? Best if you decide for yourselves, along with the BREXIT & Trump rumours amongst others!

The news in early 2019 was that the Skopje based government has ratified the proposals but do not expect that to yet be a done deal just yet.

The governmental agreement in principle is also hugely controversial in Greece with opposition parties and millions of citizens fundamentally opposed to FYROM having any claim to Macedonian history let alone the name, leading to many demonstrations throughout the country.

The biggest thorn in the average Greek's side seems to be that the language would be called Macedonian and the citizens would become Macedonians. This is a situation that is set to run for quite a while yet.

Greece also of course has a less than warm relationship with its eastern neighbours in Turkey due to centuries of occupation, artistic & religious repression, mistrust, territory grabs, wars, disputes and downright barbarism.

Therefore, as far as my extended Greek family were concerned, I had entered Greece from Konstantinopolis and was leaving for Skopje.

Scoping Skopje

The border was one of those places where you could see at first hand the haves and have-nots. Not quite as stark as Berlin after the wall came down, but a definite wealth gap was all too apparent from the quality of the houses & other buildings, as well as the likes of the cars and farm machinery on either side of the border.

These were the days before the credit crunch, when Greece was seen to be a relatively affluent EU member.

We know now of course that the country was living way beyond its means fueled by ready loans from mainly German and French banks.

In 2006 however, Greece had an economy and infrastructure that the ex-Yugoslav Republic could only dream of.

We got off the train on the FYROM side of the border as we were scheduled to be there for twenty-minutes or so for border controls.

We visited the station duty-free shop and rather than cigarettes, perfume and alcohol, the contents consisted almost entirely of electrical items like kettles, hair dryers, shavers, toasters and irons. A quite bizarre bazaar.

The train soon headed further north and arrived in Skopje on time. We had booked to stay at the once glorious Hotel Bristol. Five receptionists manned the long reception desk. We took our pick of the least surly looking.

This hotel was a real throwback, built in the '20s and not having changed very much since (although it was allegedly refurbished in 1984 having been one of the few buildings to have survived the 1963 earthquake that devastated most of the city).

It could best be described as brown. Dark wooden furniture, veneered paneling, beige wallpaper and chocolate carpets. Our room had an ancient telephone (broken) a wireless radio (not working) and a typewriter (working, but for what purpose we could not fathom).

Skopje was noticeably colder than Greece and extremely windy. We headed out for warming soup and I was pleased to see that I could understand the menu based on my basic Greek, the Cyrillic alphabet being not dissimilar to the Greek version.

We worked out our bearings. Skopje was pretty small by all accounts.

After lunch we crossed the impressive stone bridge into the Muslim quarter. There were dozens of artisan workshops surrounding a busy market. It was apparent though that there was not a great deal to do there.

We were to come to Skopje again in 2017 to find that it had changed considerably. More of that later, but let's just say that it was akin to somebody winning the lottery and going on a carefree (and pretty tasteless) spending spree.

On this first visit we paid a nominal sum to enter the city art gallery, which was impressively housed in the former hamam. The sunlight shone through the starry holes in the roof to great effect, illuminating the exhibits and seeming to bring the canvasses to life.

We were only staying for one night. Next day we would head south by bus to Lake Ohrid.

Now though, for the planned entertainment that night we would need to find a bar showing the important (to me anyway) Manchester City v Middlesbrough Premier League match.

After several knock-backs ("who is playing who", being the usual quizzical response to the question), we eventually found a place that would show it on local TV.

We arrived after a pasta dinner to find that the commentary was Slavic as expected, but unexpectedly they also had the most unusual advertising during the game.

Cars would be advertised in a unique way. A new model of a motor super-imposed being driven onto the pitch during the game, appearing to flatten players as they zoomed around the playing area.

Additionally, beer adverts consisted of rows of bottles popping up simultaneously from the bottom of the screen.

One such bottle almost obliterated City defender Richard Dunne scoring the only goal of a dire match. Hardly surprising that all I remember about the game were the adverts and the match winning header!

Not Horrid

To be honest we were not upset in leaving Skopje after such a brief stay - not an unpleasant place at all, but not that interesting either.

We caught our early morning bus for the three-and-a-half-hour journey south and were to be mightily pleased that we had chosen Ohrid for a two-night stay.

We arrived in warm midday sunshine, a distinct bonus compared with the chill we had just left behind. We walked the fifteen minutes or so from the bus station to the town and were greeted with a very pleasant centre adorned with colourful flowers & trees and plenty of lively pavement cafés to choose from.

We chose well and were rewarded with a lovely salad and a nice spot for taking in our pleasant surroundings.

The lake was a further ten-minute walk away, which was also where we would be staying. Hamish had really come up trumps with a hotel over-looking the lake itself.

We knocked but there was no reply. Just as we were both thinking that it had been too good to be true at £40 per night for a twin, a small boy of nine or ten answered the door.

Unsurprisingly he spoke no English, but had obviously been expecting us, thrusting soft white towels and a toilet roll into our arms and leading us up two flights of stairs to our bedroom.

Not only were we facing the lake, but we also had our own balcony to admire the fantastic view from. This really was a bargain. We just hoped the boy had given us the right room.

Thankfully he had as the svelte and rather attractive thirty-something owner called Vanessa confirmed fifteen minutes later, upon her return from a shopping trip.

She greeted us with another toilet roll and a request to let us know if she could help in any way. We settled on thanking her and taking countless photos of the more than pleasant view, outside across the lake rather than inside the room that is!

The sun still shone brightly, sparkling off the clear blue water, vibrantly coloured boats bobbed in the gentle breeze, a fisherman skillfully fluttered his net over the water, wildfowl flew in and landed gracefully upon the glasslike surface, geese flew serenely in V formation across the pale blue sky.

Blissful tranquility until such time as the peace was shattered by Hamish blowing his nose....

Hamish has one of those trumpeting nose blows. He does a fantastic nasal version of '76 trombones'!

Many are the times when he has blown and caused traffic to stop, crowded rooms to fall silent and dogs to run for cover.

Standing next to him when he blows ranks in between a pneumatic drill and a jumbo jet take off on the decibel scale. Hapless victims standing within earshot feel well and truly violated!

One poor American lady nearly jumped straight onto the railway tracks as we waited for our train in Myrdal, Norway during our 1992 inter-rail trip, such was her startled state caused by a nasal blast from Hamish. If looks could kill, I would have lost my travel companion before it all properly begun!

After hundreds of such experiences down the years I am just about used to it, but it certainly wakens you if your mind happens to be wandering. On this occasion, I was dreamily sailing peacefully across the lake to Albania, when a mega foghorn rudely assaulted me!

After our early start, we needed a little R&R and managed to steal a couple of hours drifting in and out of sleep whilst listening to music on our MP3s. Suitably refreshed, we decided it was time to eat.

Agreeing where to eat is rarely an issue for us and we both quickly concluded that the nearby fish restaurant was a tad pricey for our budgets, without even the need of exchanging a word on the subject.

The expensive menu we perused did give us a right laugh though as they were serving fresh crap (crab) and grilled squits (squid)! The images conjured were enough to put us off, notwithstanding the expense.

We settled on absolutely delicious mushroom lasagna and a gorgeous local red wine at a trattoria just five minutes from our hotel, followed by an early night.

Proud as a Peacock

Next morning, we took a trip a few kilometres around the lake to Sveti Nam, where a very interesting monastery was situated.

Another attraction of the place was the many peacocks that lived in the monastery grounds, including an extremely rare albino version with incredible white quills of the sort usually associated with Venetian masked balls.

He (for it was definitely a cock and not a hen) looked fantastic on all the postcards that were for sale, and as our guide leaflet explained that he lived with the common type in the monastery grounds, this was where we headed straight away.

We saw dozens of the usual blue/green varieties but Snowy was nowhere to be seen. Where could he be hiding?

We decided to buy a postcard of the red-eyed bird and ask the vendor where we could locate him. The kiosk owner understood our question through sign language and we instantly understood the response when he closed his eyes, stuck his tongue out and went limp. Snowy was no more, deceased, an ex-albino peacock!

We found out later that he had in fact died over a year before.

Obviously, the people of Sveti wanted to keep the news quiet, at least until after visitors had made the trip around the lake. For this reason, all literature about Sveti Nam still featured Snowy and just like Rod Hull's Emu, the legend lived on long after the bird could move or peck no longer!

We were of course 'heartbroken' to hear that the 'goose that laid the golden egg' had kicked the bucket, so had to amuse ourselves with a mooch around the monastery and a trip on a rowing boat along a stretch of water running off the lake.

These were stunning waters though - multi-coloured blues, greens and reds, taking the hue of the vivid plant life and colourful minerals that lay beneath the surface.

The sun shone brightly on the crystal-clear pond, also home to a variety of tiny silver and black fish. It was like floating along the top of a huge home aquarium with only the underwater bridge and miniature sunken vessel missing!

When we got back to Ohrid we decided to have a beer to toast the passing of Sveti's legendary peacock, now patiently waiting for his owner by the great rainbow bridge in the sky.

We found a nice lounge bar that was dimly lit playing melodically chilled tunes. The beer was not dark, but still went down well after a hot day peacock spotting.

Each table had a beautiful glass mosaic lantern, which added to the ambience. When I enquired, the barmaid informed me of the shop in town where I could buy such an item. I had just about enough room in my daypack to carry one, which I then had to nurse gingerly for the rest of the trip.

That evening we stuck with the mushroom lasagna and the gorgeous red. We both found room in our rucksacks for a couple of bottles too!

Busted

We were getting the early bus back next morning so got up slightly hung over at seven for breakfast on the balcony overlooking the lake, which was slowly waking up for the day just like us.

It is times like that when you appreciate being away from normality and it imprints a relaxing image to think of to help bear the daily commute or doing laborious housework when back home.

We arrived at the coach station in good time for the nine o'clock departure. The coach was waiting so we clambered aboard. There was a twenty-five-minute wait, which we wiled away watching mountains of bags being loaded into the hold and passengers struggling aboard with yet more bags.

Three minutes before the scheduled departure, the driver decided to check tickets. We handed over the return portions of ours.

Cue comical scenes. We managed to fathom that our ticket was valid for a different coach company to the one we now sat on. The next one from 'our' company left three hours later, far too late for us to get our connecting train into Serbia. Bummer!

I then made a mad dash to the ticket office, whilst the driver impatiently revved the engine. We had sat there for twenty odd minutes wasting away time and now it was Stress City Arizona!

Thankfully there were tickets available, but I had very little beans on me and even less time going by the looks of all the grim faces now obviously staring straight at me out of the coach windows.

As Hamish fidgeted embarrassed at the eyes also pointed at him like daggers, I managed to procure two single tickets at an awful € exchange rate - at least I now had enough beans from my change to buy some refreshment at the halfway stop, as well as at the train station in Skopje.

I finally stumbled aboard, head bowed to avoid the gaze of my fellow passengers. The driver took this as his signal to leave and in his determination to make back the eight- minute delay, he lurched the bus forward before I had chance to make my seat.

This sent me sprawling straight into the lap of an old lady in the process who then spontaneously shrieked like a mad witch!

A thousand apologies later, red faced and flustered, I flopped down next door to a Hamish who was now in stitches. I did not find it funny at the time, especially as the old lady and her husband were still swearing at me (or so I presumed).

After what seemed at least thirty minutes, I finally felt that nobody was looking at me at last and was able to laugh about the whole episode.

We had left Ohrid in the sunshine, but as we climbed into the hills it started to rain and before long the precipitation turned into a snow blizzard.

Our comfort break stop happened to be at our journey's highest point and we were met with a Christmas card scene with snow swirling around our heads as we descended from the coach.

After a coffee and cake, I needed the loo pretty hurriedly.

Disturbingly the café facilities were out of commission, so I had to conspicuously trudge up the hill to leave my yellow calling card*. It is hard to hide the fact that you have been for some relief when you have left a huge footprint trail leading nowhere in particular.

I had my camera out and took the odd photo to hide my guilt, but I was sure I had been tumbled by the rest of the coach's occupants. I was definitely a marked man today having first delayed the coach, then assaulted an old lady, before finally defiling some Macedonian virgin snow!

I was relieved when we finally arrived back in Skopje to catch our train to Niš in Serbia. We had hoped that our train would go through Pristina, capital of troubled Kosovo and still part of Serbia, but it however skirted around the issue, so we could not yet add another 'country' to our list.

My snowy toilet break reminded me of a favourite joke of mine – a father knocks angrily at his neighbour's door and accosts the owner when the door is opened, "your ten-year old son has written his name in pee on my snowy front lawn!"

In reply the dad of the son retorts, "Oh come on, we all did things like that as kids."

The neighbour responds irritably, "That's not what I am annoyed about, the bit that concerns me is that it is in my daughter's handwriting!"

Skopje to Niš Departure 14.35 Arrival 19.35, 205KM

A Pinch of Salt

Larger than life characters are part of life's great entertainment.

Their vivid imaginations often see them fabricating or at least embellishing, things that they have allegedly said or done.

The entertainment comes in spotting the bullshit from the truth - a case of laughing with, as well as at, the purveyor of tall tales.

Horst was just such a character and it was he that Hamish and I shared the five-hour train journey north.

So beguiling were his myths that we were tempted to stay on the train until Belgrade where Horst was headed!

Horst was in his eighties and hailed from Berlin. His permanently tanned face showed the deep lines of a life well lived, his bulbous nose the sign of bottles well drunk.

Dressed smartly in grey suit and shiny black shoes, he displayed enough bling to make pop star Goldie jealous. Thick gold chain resting on his grey-haired chest, clunky gold rings on the nicotine stained fingers of either hand, heavy gold bracelet and garish gold watch.

His grey hair was slicked back into a small ponytail - a fashion from his youth that would stay with him until the end.

'Aah, Inglisch,' he exclaimed. 'Ich like ze Inglisch despite ich bomb vem in ze var.'

We had to ask......

"Ich vas inst ze Luftwaffe und did many flies over Ingland. Dropped much bombs, shoot much airplanes. Ich vas, how you say, how you say, hero inst Deutschland. Much medals. Personal thanks from ze Fuhrer. Ich peaceful man vat love mein country. It vas duty."

That could have been a showstopper but something was not quite right. He must have been in his teens or early twenties during WWII - an unlikely fighter pilot and top gun. Hamish and I looked at each other, each with a slight grin that said bullshit in situ.

We bestowed our admiration for his brave deeds, despite the fact that our fathers had both been blitzed out of London as war refugees - information that we did not share.

Horst was ready for round two.

"After ze var ich take up to act. Vas inst much movies but ich sagt nein to offers from ze Hollywood."

I was intrigued how defeated and bankrupt Germany had moved straight back into filmmaking…….

"It vas für ………. moral (sic). Movies of peace und love. Ich habe beautiful ladies für act viff me. Much lovers. Ich vas famoose inst Deutschland, Österreich, even Svitz. Ich sleep viff Marlene"

Apparently, his early film career lasted three years but he discovered a talent for football and at twenty-eight made his debut for West Germany against Turkey. He scored two on debut but then got injured playing for Dortmund so returned to acting and presenting on German TV.

What next, politics? Correct!

"Ich become Deutsch Reagan. Vas inst Government but mein love für ze ladies ende mein kareer inst politic. Much scandal. Ich could have bin Herr Chancellor.

Since ich vas firty ich habe enough money für live forever. Since ich travel, play ze tennis, love ze women.

Ich habe biziness. Discoteks, bier halls, muzik halls. Sometimes ich sing vere. Ich still famoose inst mein homeland."

His stories were unbelievable, literally! He delivered them all with aplomb and clarity. Presumably he had delivered his tall life-story many times, so now had it down to a tee.

Perhaps he even believed them now or maybe Horst was his alter ego and he was really Fritz, a hen-pecked husband with the need for a fantasy existence to cope with the mundane.

Whatever, it made for an entertaining few hours so that the time flew by. Horst frequently left the carriage for a smoke to give us the opportunity to think of questions to ask to try and trip him up.

'Which parts of England did you bomb, who was your manager for West Germany, where did you meet Hitler, which political party were you in, how did you meet Marlene?'

Each time he answered plausibly without hesitation. Could it actually be true?

Horst was incredulous to the fact that we were visiting Niš. 'It ist, how you say, how you say, scheisshole!'

We bade him a fond farewell and said that he should visit England without his Messerschmitt. He promised he would, knowing full well that he would not.

On arriving in Niš, we felt that we were really and truly behind the old Iron Curtain. Concrete Curtain was perhaps a better description going by the amount of the stuff in evidence.

Grey concrete tower blocks, grey concrete shops and grey concrete monuments. Our huge hotel (Ambassador) was also a grey tower block and very concrete, as was the large pedestrianised square that stood before it.

Something told me that there wouldn't be much by way of entertainment here. Perhaps Horst had been accurate in his assessment?

Keeping Up Appearances

As it happened, we later stumbled across a gem of an Italian style restaurant. A warm and charming place with dark wooden panelling, exposed, polished floorboards, large chandeliers, ornate mirrors and loads of interesting photos.

It was there that we had our first ever Nikšićko dark beer, a wonderful brew from Montenegro. The beer tasted of toasted chocolate and was quite frankly the best DB (dark beer) that I had ever tasted. Hamish wholeheartedly agreed and as a member of CAMRA (it stands for Campaign for Real Ale), I trusted his judgment as being 100% correct.

(CAMRA is a British group of beer fans that extoll the virtues of independently brewed ales throughout the country and fabulous pubs to drink it in. Their virtues are to be applauded but their membership is stereotypically single blokes with beards and beer bellies!

A harsh description maybe but having attended a few CAMRA beer festivals in my time, I can vouch for the fact that a good number of their members do indeed fit at least part of that description.)

It was a smart place we frequented now and Hamish and I were the least stylish there by some distance.

We watched as a stunning and immaculately dressed lady in her early forties passed us to visit the toilet. She was a beautiful woman, over six feet tall, slender, with lovely long brunette hair. We couldn't help but follow her every move to the loo.

The toilet was the one thing that lowered the tone of the restaurant. It was slap bang in the middle of the establishment and resembled a broom cupboard. It was like Doctor Who had landed his TARDIS there and it had been later converted into a lavatory.

The gorgeous woman did not look quite so demure as she exited the cupboard to the sight of about twenty eyes gazing in her direction. A tad embarrassing!

When I was caught short thirty minutes later and had to make the same journey, I unsurprisingly had fewer eyes trained in my direction than she had endured. I was shocked to find that the toilet was of the Turkish squat variety. No wonder the beauty had lost some of her swagger!

Getting Shirty

Next day's puzzle - what to do on a full day in Niš?

A pleasant hour or so was spent in their central park with its interesting follies and its macabre monument to the Balkan Wars, a concrete wall with dozens of skulls of victims set into it.

Slightly underwhelmed it has to be said, we headed for Tramvaj for a coffee and cake (it's a middle-age thing). With no Serbo-Croat language knowledge, I managed to understand that the café's name translated to tramway and the whole place was homage to Niš's antiquated tram system.

Tram themed memorabilia was displayed everywhere and we sat in an actual tram carriage for our refreshments.

I would like to apologise in advance to my wife for the following passage.

The main shopping centre was below ground; the idea being that you could shop in comfort even when freezing winter arrived.

Hamish wanted a new belt and some photos of Mickey Mouse that he could send to his Malaysian female friend who dotes on him (Mickey not Hamish, although there is a striking resemblance). For my part I wanted a present for Mrs Wilbur.

I was drawn to buying her a shirt. Not due to the striking designs and cheap quality labels, but due to the beautiful shop assistant behind the counter of a boutique we stopped at to admire the wares.

She smiled sweetly as we entered, her eyes lighting up the low-lit shop.

She spoke almost zero English but through sign language and

pointing, I indicated that I would like to see a couple of shirts.

There were no size indications on the garments, but the thought somehow popped into my head that the slim blonde behind the till was pretty much the same size as my wife.

My next bout of sign language cheekily indicated that I would like her to put on the chosen shirt - if it fit her, it would be the right size.

Surprisingly the now giggling girl with a slight blush, agreed.

She gave us two twirls before I gave the thumbs up. She then unbuttoned the shirt right in front of us and I figured that I should get home as soon as possible for my good lady to re-enact the scene!

In the event Mrs Wilbur never wore the shirt thus denying me the opportunity to relive those Serbian memories. She gave it to a charity shop about six months later. I just hope it went to a good home.

After that we needed a DB, but as nobody seemed to stock it, we had to settle for a blonde version. Another reminder of the lovely girl we had just left as if we needed something to stir the memory further.

Having also found that no supermarkets sold Nikšićko dark, we returned to the Italian to buy some bottles for back home. Restaurant prices, but well worth the cost of a couple of bottles each. We agreed to drink them together in England at a later date.

It was then back to the hotel to re-arrange the rucksacks to ensure our bottles and glassware would be safe in transit. Unclean socks and t-shirts make excellent padded wrapping.

Later that day we were about to embark unknowingly on a journey that was impossible to forget.

Niš to Sofia Departure 11.12 Arrival 16.47, 163KM

Chilling

Our express train from Niš to Sofia had started in Belgrade and was destined for Istanbul. Having started its journey some 200 km away, it was already well over an hour late by the time it slithered into Niš.

We had waited impatiently without information with hordes of luggage laden Serbs & Bulgarians in the relative warmth of the station building, as temperatures outside fell below freezing and snow started to flit across the barren tracks.

As the weak locomotive headlights honed into view and the ancient station PA system crackled into life, downbeat but relieved passengers scrambled their possessions together and slid them purposely along the platform as the twelve-carriage train limped to a halt.

Hamish & I had been due to arrive in Sofia at teatime for a last evening hurrah before our flight home, but as we eventually set off it was very clear that the train was moving particularly slowly.

With the lack of official announcements, we soon started speculating about the actual arrival time. Predictions were pretty bleak by all accounts.

We shared our barren carriage with what appeared to be the only other English speakers on the train – a couple of Canadian girls and an American guy.

The malfunctioning train eventually crawled into the gloomy, isolated Serbian border station over three hours late. By this time, it was starting to get extremely cold and it soon became clear that the heating system had packed up.

After the palpable excitement of passport checks, we were then treated to an episode straight out of the Keystone Cops, as we moved a few metres forward out of the main station and stopped just outside in a siding.

Surrounded by razor sharp barbed wire and in the middle of absolutely nowhere, we were to stay parked up for over two and a half hours!

The train guard and driver considered it their duty to try and fix the heating for the suffering passengers, many of whom were pensioners.

Armed only with one screwdriver, some pliers and zero electrical skills, they proceeded to open every panel above the dozens of compartment doors to locate the wiring.

They then proceeded to bang and prod blindly in the forlorn hope that somehow miraculously their actions would inspire the heating to start working again.

Naturally, they were unsuccessful, the only thing their actions succeeding in doing being to make all the train lights fuse off, just to add to the air of resigned despondency that gripped the entire train.

Why they had not phoned through to Sofia to request a heating engineer and just got there as fast as possible I have no idea. At least that would have saved us nearly three hours of abject misery & boredom.

As darkness fell and the internal temperatures dropped below freezing, we were now wearing much of the contents of our rucksacks. Jumpers, scarves, hats, gloves, thick socks, fleeces. All five of us now resembled Michelin men.

I hadn't noticed that Hamish was the only one of us not to put a hat on. He was to pay for this mistake later.

I tried to speak to the guard to find out their full plan, but he did not speak even basic English, German, French or Greek, so we remained totally in the dark in more ways than one.

The cold and gloomy conditions at least got us talking to our companions. Food was shared by torchlight, travel stories told, and jokes concocted about our current predicament.

We even resorted to riddles to keep ourselves entertained, for example I set a conundrum.

"A man walks into a pub and requests a glass of water. The barman reaches for a gun and points it at the man. The man momentarily freezes before saying thank you very much and leaving the bar happy. Why was he so thankful?" *

* The man had hiccups

After a couple of false starts we finally left. No heat or light, but at least we were moving. The whole train cheered.

The train was still travelling way below optimum pace and we were now over five hours late.

The five of us had all run out of food, conversation and any inspiration by the time we finally crawled into Sofia an excruciating six hours late.

The train still had to get to Istanbul, another 550 kilometres away. We felt really sorry for the two unsuspecting old ladies that we saw board as we alighted. At this rate it could be days before they reached Turkey! There was no sign of any heating engineers either.

We bade our fellow travellers farewell and went off in search of a taxi to take us to our reserved hotel. It was now after 11 o'clock, so all notion of a last night jolly was blown out of the water.

There was no signage to speak of at Sofia Central, so we went off in search of a taxi rank in what we thought was roughly the right direction.

The North Americans went to the main concourse to try and arrange some accommodation. I wished them luck, whilst Hamish remained strangely silent.

It was then that I properly realised that Hamish was struggling somewhat. He had got so cold that his lips were blue, and he was shivering uncontrollably. The early stages of hypothermia had set in - we needed to find somewhere warm quickly.

We staggered up some steps and found ourselves stood beside a six-lane highway that now separated us from the train station.

The taxi rank was infuriatingly by the station across the carriageway. We were just about to walk back down the steps when I noticed a taxi driving by, which I exuberantly flagged down by waving my arms furiously in the air.

It did the trick and thankfully the driver knew where our hotel was and agreed to take us there. We slumped onto the back seat where I listened to Bulgarian radio accompanied by the chattering of Hamish's teeth.

After fifteen minutes we stopped and the taxi driver lazily gestured that our hotel was somewhere on the left through a pedestrian zone. Beanless, I quickly found a cashpoint to draw some Lev, but by the time I returned Hamish had already settled up with a €2 coin.

We slumped off in the general direction indicated by Mr Taxi in search of our hotel. I could see that Hamish was in a pretty bad way, so when we stumbled across an Italian restaurant, I ushered him inside - the hotel could wait.

A pizza and some red wine later and the world seemed an infinitely better place.

Our waiter knew our hotel and offered to lead us there, an offer we were grateful to accept.

When we arrived, we were dismayed to find that they had treated us as a 'No Show' and given our room away. Fortunately, they had a sister hotel that had a twin-room free. A taxi was ordered and we eventually arrived there around 1 in the morning.

The hotel receptionist was curled up on a sofa asleep so had to be woken to take our booking. She had looked so cute that we were reluctant to awaken her but needs dictated that we had to.

The pair of us had to be up again in four hours or so for our flight home, but still had to go through the ritual of handing over our passports for photocopying.

We arranged for the same taxi driver to meet us at six to take us to the airport.

Barely awake enough to be able to get undressed, we were soon sound asleep and stayed that way until the evil alarm clock blasted out its rallying call at 05.30. Bastard!

Footnote - all glassware made it home unscathed and the ornate lantern from Ohrid still stands proudly in our dining room. Mrs Wilbur and I enjoyed the bottle of red a week later whilst Hamish and I relived the holiday just before Christmas with a photo sideshow and the wonderful Nikšićko beers.

Chapter Four – No Beards
(October 2007)

Albania had always been a mystical place to us, Europe's outcast being neither East nor West.

During our teenage years we used to try and get information about the place, but in those Internet free days this was hard to come by.

We knew that beards were banned, we knew it was Communist, we knew of the former royal ruler, the wonderfully named King Zog, we knew the country loved British comic legend Norman Wisdom, but very little else.

In those days, there were no flights in from Western Europe and no international train connections, although it might have been possible to sail there from Greece or Italy as long as none of the crew had more than a whisker of facial hair. Captain Birdseye would have been a real no go!

It was not part of the inter-rail network for obvious reasons, so an enigma it was to remain in every way to our curious minds.

We were determined to get there one day though and finally managed it in 2007.

By that time Enver Hoxha, who had ruled the country with an iron fist for forty-one years, had died. Hoxha had purposely kept Albania isolated for much of his autocratic reign, in a very similar way to the modern-day leaders of equally enigmatic North Korea.

Initially his regime was allied to the Soviet Union, but fell out with the Kremlin and so sought friendly relations with China. Once these ties were also cut Albania went it alone, staying self-sufficient and largely undeveloped.

Hoxha's death in 1985 saw a lightening of the austere regime that controlled the lives of most Albanians. However, in a similar way to Tito's death in Yugoslavia, the removal of the iron fist led to other issues such as corruption, political in-fighting and violent public demonstrations.

Albania shot to European infamy once more in the late '90s when its national savings scheme collapsed leaving millions of its citizens flat broke and leading to more riots, demonstrations and eventually reform.

The subsequent comparative stability persuaded British Airways to introduce a direct flight to Tirana in 2006 and the dream was on.

Arriving at Tirana Airport was like a date with destiny. Alighting the plane, I looked up to see the Tirana sign illuminated in large red letters above the arrival hall. My heart jumped for joy, we were finally actually here.

We arrived in our small hotel just off the main square and immediately headed off in search of DB.

We had no local beans and neither of us had the foresight to check the exchange rate so we had absolutely no idea how many Albanian Lek there were to the Pound.

Hamish took the plunge at the ATM, not sure whether he had withdrawn £3 or £300*.

On the basis that the beers came to 50% of what he had drawn, we sincerely hoped that it was a lot closer to the former number.

The DB was called Korça, and what a splendid brew it was too. So much so that we invested the rest of the beans on a second.

* It transpired that Hamish had drawn the equivalent of £2.73 and been charged £3.80 for the privilege. We figured that to be a fair price for four Korças!

Big Cat Diary

Next morning, we took breakfast in the sunny garden courtyard of the hotel. They had a menagerie of birds in cages and bizarrely two chipmunks. Their pen was far too small we thought as we munched our bread and jam.

"We are in Albania!" I exclaimed, still not quite believing we had made it to this land of mystique. "We bloody well are!" came Hamish's enthusiastic response.

We were to be in Tirana for four nights before heading for Shkodra in the North of the country and from there into Montenegro. We hatched our plans.

Today we would discover the capital; next day would feature a train trip to the coastal city of Durres. Day three would see us off down South to Berati. We would also fit in Skanderbeg's Castle somewhere along the way.

Plans subsequently got juggled somewhat and we ended up staying an extra night for a special reason that will be revealed – such is the flexibility of independent travel.

It was t-shirt weather and I proudly wore my Norman Wisdom number, freshly procured for the trip. I thought it might be a handy icebreaker.

Skanderbeg Square is the central hub of Tirana, surrounded by a wide traffic strewn roundabout (or so it was in 2007, but has now been radically redeveloped as we were to discover with more than a little disappointment in 2017) and home to the central mosque, clock tower, national museum, the opera house and a domineering statue of Albanian hero Skanderbeg on horseback (all still intact in 2017 gladly).

It is also the site of several government buildings, Tirana's only 'international' business hotel and some water-free fountains (now also gone), possibly as they would just have been used as a bathroom facility going by the number of unsavory characters in situ.

The square was a real social hub. Old men played chess or just hanging out, children rode toy vehicles that you could hire on site and the youth crowd shared topical information. Nobody seemed to notice my t-shirt though.

Perhaps I should have worn a George W Bush one (also an Albanian hero for his support for Albanian majority Kosovo in their efforts to gain independence from Serbia). In retrospect there was no way I could bring myself to sport Dubya on my chest.

Just as we contemplated what to do with our day, we simultaneously clocked a spectacle that had us chuckling merrily and still raises a smile whenever mentioned to this day.

An old and battered silver estate car pulled up and parked right in front of us. A grey-haired man in a scruffy blue jacket got out and went to his boot from which he pulled a huge replica stuffed toy tiger, complete with fixed a menacing growl.

Balancing the replica feline on his shoulders, he then took his Polaroid from the front seat and promptly marched to his position in the heart of the square.

For a few beans you could have your photo taken with the big cat look alike. Amazingly many people did. We are still kicking ourselves that we did not.

We speculated how the guy had been left a few quid in his parent's will and had pondered for days about how he could invest the money to secure his future.

Wisely he hadn't gone for one of the doomed saving schemes and had instead ploughed his good fortune into an instant camera and a less than lifelike toy.

It seemed to be working for him, so you had to admire his acumen!

As you are aware, Hamish and I do not usually do museums together, but this was to be a rare exception. The Lonely Planet guidebook (LP for short) proclaimed it as a must see, not for ancient pots and vases, but to give a perspective of the suppressed life under Hoxha.

So, we paid our money and learned all about how Albania became Muslim (to avoid paying tax to their Ottoman overlords apparently) and what life was like under the murderous regime (no access to the outside world, with the crime of owning a radio carrying the death penalty).

The museum housed a complete prison cell that used to cram several inmates at a time in its tiny space. Apparently, life here was more austere than any of the Eastern Bloc countries.

We also learned the story of all the strange little bunkers that are dotted about the country.

Convinced that his country was going to be invaded, Hoxha ordered a bizarre building project that saw around seven hundred thousand concrete bunkers constructed as a method of national defence, the idea being that civilians would arm themselves and defend the Albanian nation from attack.

Apparently Hoxha asked the chief engineer of the prototype construction whether the bunker would be able to withstand a tank attack. When he replied with certainty that it would, the engineer was then ordered into the bunker and promptly had it driven over several times by a huge armoured vehicle. Thankfully for the engineer he was proved correct in his assertion.

The foreign invasion never came, and after the fall of the Communist regime the bunkers lost their military use. They are now used for many purposes such as living quarters, animal shelters, cafés and store rooms.

Thousands survive situated in locations from mountains to countryside to beaches, many of which have been painted in vivid colours to brighten up the original grey bland concrete.

We read fully with interest the reason that Albania became majority Muslim. Ruled by the Ottomans from 1478-1912, they encouraged conversion to the Islamist faith from Christianity by introducing arbitrary taxes to all non-Muslims.

Despite this, it took almost four centuries to convince enough citizens to switch religions to give the Islamic faith the official majority in the country.

The Communist Hoxha regime actually declared Albania as the world's first and only 'Atheist State', with believers facing harsh punishments and many religious clergy persecuted or killed. Albania has been constitutionally a secular country since 1967.

The final fascinating fact that we learned was that unbeknown to us at that time, Mother Teresa of Calcutta was part Albanian. In 2001 they named the main international airport after Saint Teresa, a handy hint for future generations as to her 'nationality'.

Teresa was actually born as Agneza Gonxha Bojaxhiu in Skopje in 1910 (then part of the Kosovo Vilayet of the Ottoman Empire) to Albanian & Indian parents.

It won't surprise you to learn that Macedonia also (perhaps justifiably) claims credit for the world's most famous Roman Catholic nun, as evidenced by the rather gaudy Skopje monument known as the Mother Teresa Memorial House, that sprang up during the city's 'glorification' period that has been on-going since 2010, as you will read about in chapter nine.

She in fact left Macedonia when aged 18 to move to Ireland and from there onto India where she spent most of her life.

Nationality wasn't a straightforward thing in the Balkans in her early life, with her being alternately Ottoman, Serbian, Bulgarian and Yugoslavian, before taking Indian citizenship in 1950 and dual Albanian citizenship in 1991.

Suitably educated, we set about exploring after a coffee at the 'imaginatively' named International Hotel on King Zog Boulevard. Still nobody recognised Norman or were too shy to say anything, so I asked Hamish for a rare photo of me standing with a ferocious looking Skanderbeg as a fitting background.

To be honest, the square was pretty much it for Tirana sightseeing. Once we had toured the mosque, there was not a lot else to do but stroll and watch the locals go about their daily lives. We were not really there to see heritage anyway - just being there was enough for us.

As we crossed Skanderbeg Square, I was the victim of a hit and run!

A kid of about four was going like the clappers in his pedal car, but was not exactly in control of the steering. The youngster rode straight over my foot, painfully clipping my ankle at the same time.

As the brat rode off without a care in the world, I yelped half in surprise and half in pain.

The audibility of my cry seemed to stop the square dead. The tiger man put down his giant toy, pedalling kids braked (apart from my ignorant assailant that is), old men silenced their conversations & delayed their next chess move, mums quit gossiping and the small handful of tourists let their cameras rest.

Everybody seemed to be staring at the foreign nutter now crouched down nursing his battered foot.

Hamish went from initial (apparent) concern to laughter in what seemed a nano-second, whilst I checked that no bones were broken. Luckily, there were not, but below my sock I could see that my ankle was already turning red.

The crowd continued to gawp as I limped across to an empty bench to gingerly remove my shoe and sock. No real damage, except now to my ego. Why was I the one that was embarrassed, the hapless victim?

I glowered towards the little hooligan that had caused my pain and ignominy. He was now badgering his forlorn looking mother for some sweets or an ice cream. The post Hoxha generation!

The square had returned to its usual busy self as I applied half a tube of antiseptic cream to my injury.

It was high time for a DB to get over my ordeal. I did consider an accidental arm to the ear of the careless driver as I limped past, but wisely figured that this may end in tears for us both, so avoided the temptation.

We noted the Buda bar as a venue for later on and then decided to head for the hills and Skanderbeg's castle after we had devoured a quick Korça & chips.

There's Rain in Them Thar Hills

Summoning a taxi, we were soon heading upwards. This was only after we agreed to pay double price so that the taxi driver would stop waiting for his other two seats to be filled before we departed.

This still didn't stop him picking up others en route and charging them; even though it meant we needed to make a timewasting detour to take them exactly where they wanted to go. A good job we had agreed a fixed price!

As we climbed the steep hill, the weather changed and by the time we got to the village just below the castle, it had turned to monsoon type precipitation, quickly followed by cherry sized hail.

Bugger, we now had to get out of the taxi and neither of us had a coat. After thirty seconds debate, we decided against just going back to the capital, so paid our dues and managed to dive into a nearby grocer shop that doubled as a café, just about avoiding a drenching in the process.

I actually tackled the slippery surface with greater aplomb than Hamish, who very nearly came a cropper.

It is so satisfying when ungainly me out-balances anybody. I can usually do more than a passing (and unintentional) impression of Monty Python's Ministry of Funny Walks!

As we supped our lemon tea and watched the rain pouring off the canopy, we contemplated how to get out of this soggy mess. Our taxi had departed and there was no way we were walking further up the hill in the downpour.

As the last drops of tea passed our lips, the rain eased enough for us to brave it.

Just down from the castle a narrow street full of souvenir shops was situated. We were not in the market for anything but decided to browse whilst the rain eased further (or so we hoped).

It did the trick and by the time we exited the stamp and coin shop, the sky was blue and the sun shining. Hamish actually bought some ancient coins, no idea why, perhaps an offering to the sun god.

The castle was pretty nondescript, merely a ramshackle collection of outbuildings, a small chapel and a museum. Unbelievably for the second time that day we were to visit a museum!

And pretty good it was too. All about Skanderbeg and his army, the defenders against the Ottoman Turk invaders. Weaponry and tales of heroism are far more interesting than cracked terracotta.

Hamish did his usual photo frenzy (he is bloody good at it actually) before we headed back down to the village. Luckily, we quickly found a taxi to take us back to Tiger Bay, as we now called the main square.

The photographer was just packing up his replica Shere Khan and putting away his camera. His smile told us he had had a profitable day. Why the heck didn't we have that picture taken!?

That night was a big night. We were going to Buda Bar and it was also the Rugby Union World Cup semi-final between France and England in Paris.

I had watched England's famous and unexpected win in the quarterfinal against Australia on TV the previous weekend and then attended France's equally unexpected win against New Zealand in Cardiff.

No chance of watching the game in rugby (and Irish bar) free Tirana, but I had been promised text score updates at regular intervals from JC, my rugby loving mate.

Onto Buda Bar, a poor imitation of the Parisian version of Buddha Bar, but an apt venue for me to cheer on England against their Gallic hosts.

No Korça (far too trendy for that), so a delightful red was a more than able substitute. Two bottles later we were hopelessly drunk. I was giddy also on the tension and excitement of a narrow England victory against all the odds. Our boys were losing with five minutes to go but scored two late penalties for a 14-9 victory.

The tension was lost on Hamish who can just about master the laws of football and cricket (apart from offside and Leg Before Wicket) and has no time for the oval ball game.

He was also far too pre-occupied by the group of good-looking young ladies in the far corner drinking champagne. Bright young Albanian things with money. Very alluring.

The bar itself followed the Buddha rule of being just about lit enough to see your hand, but even in the gloom we could see that these ladies were way out of our league, even if we had been interested in some unbecoming flirtatious behaviour. They were Premier Division to our Southern League fifth XI status. It is free to dream however!

We could see that they were smoking a water pipe and we decided we should do likewise.

We had done it once before in Jordan and back then, as non-smokers, we ended up like giggling schoolboys after half a cider.

It was only apple tobacco, but once more it did the business. We were now floating high above the giant golden statue of Buddha and laughing incessantly.

It was time to leave. The 'it-crowd' may have thought of us as quite cool travellers a while before, but would now be firmly of the opinion that we were just juvenile tourists. Darn, cover blown!

Somehow, we staggered back to the hotel and awoke some hours later with thrashing hangovers. We would not be joining Chip n' Dale for breakfast that morning!

Berated in Berati

Today was our trip to Berati, the town of a thousand windows, so called for all the Ottoman style houses that clung to the hillside. Still feeling the worse for wear, we boarded the bus for the journey south.

The pot holed roads and crazy road users made the ride a stop-start and continually uncomfortable affair. Just what the doctor didn't order. This had the effect of stirring last night's excesses with that morning's banana and coffee breakfast. Not a great combo.

When we finally arrived, I was far from peak condition. Annoyingly Hamish was fresh and chirpy. The bus dropped us in the main square next to a man walking his giant sow. Like you do!

Berati was a pleasant place, split in two by the River Osum. A farmer ably steered his horse and hay laden cart over the river bridge, turning the tightest of angles without dropping so much as a single stalk. His load virtually filled the bridge's narrow width making passing impossible - it all had a distinctly rural charm.

We soon bumped into a Kiwi who had been backpacking for a fortnight. These were the days before smart phones and land-to-sky WIFI, so I delighted in bringing him up to date on the rugby.

He simply could not believe that New Zealand had lost to France and I must admit to taking pleasure in relaying in detail the events of their demise. They had been so cocksure of winning the trophy.

I had actually attended the match in Cardiff with my mad Welshman mate known to all as Evans. The Southern Hemisphere side had raced into a 13-nil lead in double quick time but the French came back to secure an unlikely and hard-fought 17-13 victory.

A feather in the cap of the Northern Hemisphere as the tournament favourites were defeated, helping to set up my nervy evening the night before.

After the momentary return of brightness and well-being, I soon deteriorated again. We were due to yomp up the hill to the castle and the many churches above the houses. Hamish would have to go alone and relay his findings. I was officially as sick as a dog.

So, the big-eared traveller headed up hill while the long-necked lightweight slumped at the kafeneio. Hopefully coke and rest would be the cure.

I had visited neighbouring Greece on dozens of occasions and the mentality of the Albanians seemed remarkably similar to what I witnessed there.

This establishment was a male only bastion, a meeting place for young and old alike. Greek coffee, cigarettes, backgammon, worry beads and chauvinism.

I observed for ninety-minutes and was momentarily transported to an Athens suburb.

Raucous laughter, back slapping, story-telling and (assumed on my part) bad language.

Whilst sat at the café I witnessed a cruel episode, in my easily offended English opinion anyway, which spoiled my mood further.

What can only be described as the village idiot came along. A boy in his late teens or early twenties, snub-nosed, buck-toothed and clearly a few islands short of an archipelago.

The men continued to twirl their worry beads as they mercilessly toyed with the poor unfortunate. He was encouraged to do his donkey impression that saw him on all fours braying wildly through his protruding gnashers.

The sight of his spittle dribbling down the front of his filthy t-shirt did nothing for my queasy stomach. His shirt had evidently once been pale blue, but now bore the souvenirs of his every meal of the past six months or so. Disgusting!!

One of the tormentors tossed the wretch a lit cigarette or at least the dying remains of one. The delighted youth scrabbled in the dirt to retrieve the burning butt and arose triumphantly with it pursed between his scabby lips.

The men laughed at such 'comedy', laughter that only heightened when he started choking on the smoke.

The poor kid was then dispatched to buy cigarettes for the merciless group. A brief respite for him and this horrified Englishman.

He soon returned with the contraband - his reward for his errand being a clip round the ear for some misdemeanour that one of the mob had determined he had perpetrated.

The pattern was broken when a very attractive girl of around eighteen entered the scene. She became the subject of the male attentions, the group guffawing crudely as no doubt sexist comments were fired towards the young woman.

With long black hair, lightly perspiring bronzed skin, alluring red lips and cobalt blue eyes, she positively shimmered in the sunshine. I imagined her to be the spitting image of the 'Girl from Ipanema'.

She was about five foot six and of slim build and dressed in yellow mini skirt and white blouse tied above the belly button to reveal her perfectly toned midriff. She also wore large hoop silver earrings that gleamed brightly. She was undeniably a beauty and clearly enjoyed the attention she was attracting.

I figured that her astounding looks were not matched in the brains department and feared that she too was purely there for the pleasure of the chauvinists.

She was soon beckoned over to the table and poured a large brandy, which she downed in one - I could stand it no longer. I was sure she was being buttered up for carnal desires.

I forgot my illness, stood up sharply sending my chair crashing to the floor and exclaimed loudly, "FOR FUCK SAKE!!"

All eyes were now on me. I had no follow up in me, however. Dizzy from the abrupt rise and my malcontent, I had to let it rest there.

The café owner came to rescue my embarrassed predicament, as luck would have it. He had realised that the men had gone too far and fearing that I may report what I had seen (I undoubtedly wouldn't have), he shouted at the partially inebriated rabble.

Looks turned away from me and towards the proprietor. More angry words were exchanged before the men dispersed muttering loudly as they left, once their glasses had been emptied of course.

The pretty girl seemed perplexed, whilst the retarded youth started howling uncontrollably like a demented wolf. A smack around the head administered by the young siren silenced the din and they left together in the direction the men had just followed.

It appeared that they were sister and in-bred brother as they wandered off into the distance arm in arm. I really hoped that they were not just off to start all over again at some other establishment about town, but sadly I expected that to be what would happen.

As I sat there stewing in the heat of early afternoon, I concluded that there was no way that I could bus it back. I would pay for a taxi whatever the cost.

Just as I wondered what to do now, my roaming buddy returned ready to regale his exerts. He was instead transfixed as I relayed the events of the last thirty minutes, especially so as I described the young temptress.

He barely touched his beer for the duration such was his wonderment. When it was time to leave, we happily found that the drinks had been on the house. The owner really was concerned it seemed.

Hamish sportingly agreed that a taxi would be better and agreed to share the cost. This would be just €20 for the eighty kilometre journey.

I had the back seat to myself and despite the rough road I managed to sleep for almost the entire journey.

Hamish did start to tell me how good the castle had been, but to be honest I did not really care at that moment and soon drifted off to images of gorgeous gypsy girls, the toreador song from Carmen as background soundtrack to the vision.

The power nap did me a world of good and I felt almost back to prime condition by the time we were dropped off. DB was not on the menu, but I was certainly ready to eat. I took that as a welcome sign of my imminent recovery.

Karma in Kosovo

As already mentioned, George W Bush is a hero in Albania due to the support he gave to the Kosovars in their quest for independence.

Kosovo is home to a majority of ethnic Albanians and Bush's support for their brothers made him universally popular in Tirana and beyond.

Kosovo's independence all seemed to hinge on the results of the Serbian elections of 2006, their first since Montenegro had left the union.

If the hard liner anti-West candidate were re-elected president, the gloves would come off. However, if the pro-West reformer won, it was thought a blind eye would be turned, and no blood would be shed.

The latter result came about with Boris Tadić elected president and Kosovo got its way, well almost.

They declared themselves independent in 2008, but at the time of writing Serbia have never ratified their full independence, so Kosovo has yet therefore to be welcomed categorically into the United Nations.

This is the official determining factor as to whether a nation truly exists, even though influential countries such as the USA and UK, do recognise Kosovo as a de facto state and lately so do sporting organisations such as Football's FIFA and the International Olympic Committee.

Back in 2007 it was considered safe to proceed with caution if travelling from friendly neighbours Albania. For many years this was not the case of course as capital Pristina, and Kosovo as a whole, became synonymous with the brutal ethnic cleansing and battles of the Yugoslav conflict.

With a relative peace prevailing and as we were so close we thought we should try and go, so had struck a deal the previous evening with a taxi driver to take us to the city of Prizren and back for $50. Hotel pick up was arranged for 07.30.

It would take about four and a half hours each way, so we decided we could spend a couple of hours in the city and still get back in time for dinner and DB.

If I am honest, the trip was more about bragging rights in telling friends we had been to Kosovo, but in the event we found the place well worth the visit, even though it did turn into an absolute marathon.

The quoted journey times turned out to be not quite fact! We made the border in the four and a half hours we were told it would take to complete the entire journey and then had another hour to get across the border controls.

We were still officially entering Serbia according to the Serbs, so we had also been advised to avoid a Kosovar stamp in our passports if we ever wanted to visit Belgrade (which we did).

It took a bit of hand signalling and insistence, but eventually we got our way. From the border it was another ninety-minutes to Prizren, meaning we did not arrive until 14.30, a total of seven hours!

It turned out that the four and a half hours that had been mentioned was indeed the time to the border and not the entire journey. Sign language and pidgin English were clearly not good for mutual understanding.

If we had known we would have been car bound for fourteen hours, I am pretty certain we would not have bothered, but at least the scenery was stunning in many places on the way.

We decided we wanted to see as much as possible having come all this way, but were also starving hungry.

We therefore started in Sadirvan, a touristic spot with plenty of restaurants to choose from. We sat outside in the early afternoon sunshine, near the historic water fountain.

As I supped my coke and ate my salad whilst stretching the cramp out of my legs, I started to wish we were staying here the night.

The lunch spot was tranquil and the beautiful setting of the place, surrounded by brooding mountains, merited a longer stay.

Trying to block out the seven-hour journey back was also largely behind this thought I am certain!

After lunch, we whizzed around the compact city and saw pretty much all the sites (externally anyhow) in around an hour. The stone bridge, the Serbian Orthodox Monastery, Sinan Pasha Mosque and its less impressive relatives.

Finally, we route-marched up to the castle to enjoy some excellent views of the leafy city below.

It was now five in the afternoon and time to go if we were to get back by midnight. We had bought a few supplies (they accepted Albanian beans everywhere), so had a beer (blonde unfortunately), some crackers and some crisps for the journey back.

We figured we would sleep for a good part of the return, but were a little concerned about Jak, our driver, who would surely be knackered by the end of his shift.

As night fell, we arrived at the border and handed over our passport with the stamped paper. The paper was taken and we were waved through – it was like we had never set foot in Kosovo at all.

It had only taken thirty minutes at border control to get back into Albania – perhaps we would be back in time for last orders after all.

We decided to celebrate by cracking open our still fairly cold beers. We hit a snag however as Hamish had left the bottle opener back at the hotel.

Jak spied our predicament through the rearview mirror and shouted, "no problem". He pulled over and beckoned us to hand the bottles over. He then proceeded to pull a large knife out of the glove compartment and skillfully used it to prise the tops from our beers.

We looked at each other open-mouthed, not due to the dexterity that Jak had displayed, but due to the fact that he had taken a lethal weapon over a border without giving it a moment's thought.

Different standards and perhaps in Jak's mind we had never actually left Albania.

We supped our beers and ate our fodder as we contemplated the sabre that now lay back in the glove compartment.

This put us off the idea of sleep somewhat, even though Jak seemed like a great guy. In fact, sleep would have been pretty impossible anyway due to Jak playing loud folk music and having his window wound right down to help keep himself alert.

Worse than this, the road was extremely pot-holed and whereas we had been able to skirt around the worst bits on the outward journey, this was far trickier in the darkness, meaning we constantly had to brake or wait for on-coming traffic to pass before it was safe for us to proceed.

Jak naturally smoked like a chimney and needed two coffee breaks to help him keep his eyes open (and for us to have a pee).

All in all, the journey was stop-start all the way and very uncomfortable indeed throughout (bit of an Albanian theme it seemed).

It actually took us eight hours to get back. Fifteen hours of travelling for little more than two hours at the destination. This was even worse than when I used to drive from my Devon home for ninety-minutes of (usually dire) football in Manchester watching City.

Tirana was dead at one in the morning and we needed to rouse our receptionist to let us in. Jak earned $70 from us with a tip; he was delighted but had earned it all right.

Crawling into bed knackered, all thoughts were on sleeping for a long time. However, next day we had a train to catch to the seaside.

Footnote 1 – in 2013 the Albania-Kosovo expressway opened and you can now do the journey we undertook in just over two hours. We were to do just that in 2017.

Footnote 2 – in October 2014, Serbia played Albania in an international football match, having been drawn in the same Euro qualification group. This was recognised as a powder keg of a game, so Albanians were banned from travelling to Belgrade to watch.

This did not stop an unknown entity stationed outside the ground from flying a drone into the stadium and over the pitch with a flag of 'Greater Albania' hanging from it. The flag showed Kosovo and Albania as one enlarged nation, causing fury in the ground.

A Serbian player grabbed the flag, enraging their opponents. Soon all hell broke loose, players squaring up to

107

each other and hooligan fans entering the field of play to aim kicks and punches at the Albanian players.

The Albanians fled down the players tunnel under a barrage of jeers and projectiles to the safety of the dressing room. Unsurprisingly the game was abandoned.

This just goes to show how emotive the whole Kosovo issue still is and how inept UEFA was for not keeping the nations apart in the qualifying group.

Albania were subsequently awarded the game, which in turn helped them to qualify for their first ever major football championship finals.

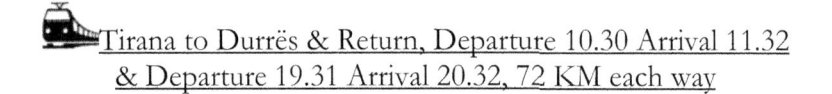

Tirana to Durrës & Return, Departure 10.30 Arrival 11.32 & Departure 19.31 Arrival 20.32, 72 KM each way

Following our Kosovo adventure, we were off to Durrës, Albania's second largest city, situated on the Adriatic Sea. This meant we would travel on one of Albania's few train lines.

Tirana's train station was a totally ramshackle affair. Its main building was dilapidated and the platforms full of potholes that had filled with rainwater.

Rusted machinery, wrecks of discarded carriages and old locomotives that were long since past their sell by date, littered the railway sidings and battled with the weeds for dominance.

A huge Czech-built ČKD diesel-electric locomotive would pull us. Evidently its size did not equate to power, as we crawled along at thirty KMH. This may seem sedentary, but imagine when the railway first arrived as late as 1947. Albanians, used to travelling by horse and cart, would have been amazed.

The train itself was ancient by most country's standards, built neither for comfort nor speed. Bone hard plastic seats and with every window cracked, apparently the result of errant kids with rocks.

We also got our first sighting of the mushroom like shelters of the like we had viewed in the museum, scattered across the landscape like measles.

These were all of the neglected grey concrete variety rather than the converted types. We were to see one later on the trip that had been painted red with white dots to resemble a giant toadstool of the like you see in British woods.

Mistaken identity

The hour-long journey had seen me strike up proper conversation with an Albanian for the first time.

He 'recognised' my Norman Wisdom t-shirt. "Aah, Benny Hill, very funny," he knowingly asserted.

I explained that although Benny Hill was indeed very funny, that the image I displayed was of a different comic genius. He had never heard of Norman, Pitkin or Mr. Grimshaw. A myth crushed perhaps?

The man was in his seventies and spoke good English. He had only learned the language post Hoxha from reading children's English learning books and listening to the BBC.

He was now on to French, again with a children's book, which he was reading on the journey whilst writing notes in an exercise book.

The rest of the journey turned into a French vocabulary test, my schoolboy French losing out to his pensioner version, much to his delight.

We eventually crawled into Durrës Central, a small station with two operational platforms. Happily, the local kids had decided against target practice that day so we had not had to duck any flying debris.

I bade farewell to 'Old John' (or Ancient Jean as he now liked to be called) and we headed to the beach area.

We tried to imagine the place thronging with tourists, something hard to picture on this cold October day. The sea and sky were dull grey whilst the beach was shingle, bordered by a wide expanse of grey concrete. Only the odd palm tree interrupted the barren scene.

This was very much like winter in Sidmouth - not very inspiring. Mind you, that could be said of Sidmouth any time of the year and certainly appeared also true of Durrës. A kiddie's merry-go-round was being covered up; the meagre fun had been sucked away for the season.

There had been the promise of viewing the ancient Roman amphitheatre, but unfortunately this had also shut up shop for the Winter, leaving us with just a peek through some corrugated iron hoardings to satisfy our admittedly slight archeological gene.

With nothing to detain us very long, we sauntered into the town in search of a place that may be showing England's World Cup qualifier against Estonia. After several failures and much to our surprise we found a café that could show the match and they agreed to do so.

I was proud to see that the right flank of the England team for the game came straight out of Manchester City's youth academy, with young right-back Micah Richards and right-winger Shaun Wright-Philips, who by then was playing for Chelsea.

I was even prouder when Wright-Phillips put England one up early on. He may have been playing for a rival club at that time, but he was and always will be a City fan's favourite (he was actually to return to City in 2009 amid great excitement).

That was pretty much the last action we saw. The screen packed up and nobody could fix it. Nowhere else had a satellite, as we had found out in our earlier fruitless search.

England cantered to a comfortable three-nil win as it happened, to set up a crunch qualifier in Russia the following Wednesday, a match we planned to see in Montenegro.

At least we had the compensation of a DB to counter the frustration of the non-functioning satellite link.

After the beer we had a quick look around the town. Those days CD shops were still magnets for us and we purchased a few bootlegs for less than £1 each.

Before parting with the money, we made the shop owner play some sample tracks from each disc on the giant ghetto blaster that filled the counter area, to test the quality. A practice we probably would not have dreamed of insisting on back home.

A further DB with our pizza meant that we fell asleep on the crawl back to Tirana. At thirty KMH, the train was like a giant gently rocking cradle and it didn't take much persuasion for us to drift off.

We sleep walked off the train and back to the first bar we had visited for a last DB in the Albanian capital. We decided that aesthetically Tirana was a pretty nondescript place, except for the vital fact that it was Tirana, that magical, mystical place that could only be imagined in our youth.

🚆 Tirana to Shkodra Departure 13.15 Arrival 16.42, 98KM

Lake District

We bade a fond farewell to Tirana, stopping off at a local supermarket to stuff as many Korças as we could manage into our rucksacks - a princely five each!

Today's crawl would be a longer one – three and a half hours for the journey north towards the border with newly independent Montenegro.

We planned to stay one night in Shkodra, a small city near Albania's biggest lake.

The place turned out to be incredibly boring, just a stop off on our journey. Furthermore, there was no DB on offer anywhere, a fact that would have tainted even a UNESCO World Heritage city, let alone a bland place like this.

It seemed a waste to open one of our Korças, not even considering the fact that to try and explain to a bar that we would like them to put two of our bottles in their fridge for us to consume thirty minutes hence. would have been a task well beyond us.

The castle on the outskirts of town was quite impressive (we viewed it from the road on the way out) and the interior of the mosque was nice and colourful, but that was about your lot.

I am undoubtedly being unfair. If we had been into hiking or bird watching, this would have been the perfect base to explore the area. The surrounding region did sound very pleasant with the lakes and the Albanian Alps, but we had no time to explore there.

So, an uneventful evening was spent with a pizza and a blonde beer. Our only 'entertainment' being an episode of Albania's equivalent of Top of the Pops showing on the café TV.

The programme transported us straight back to '70s England and the likes of dance group Pam's People wearing flares and power shoulders, The Tavares showing off their bushy sideburns and presenter Tony 'Tight Trousers' Blackburn excitedly counting down the top 40.

It was back to our dull hotel, a quick nightcap in the dull hotel bar and off to bed by ten. Yawn.

Road Trip

We arose bright an early next day to plot our way out. This was the end of the train line so we would need wheels to get us over the border into Montenegro.

A fee was agreed with a middle-aged taxi driver to take us over the border to Bar, where we could catch a train to take us further afield.

We sat in the back and off we went. Our chauffeur spoke to somebody on his mobile and promptly took us to a housing estate, got out of the car and disappeared.

He seemed friendly, but it was a little disconcerting. He spoke no English, but we hoped he had nipped home to collect something for the journey rather than setting us up for something nasty.

When he reappeared a few minutes later, a beautiful young lady accompanied him. Had he got the wrong end of the stick? As beautiful as the girl was, we were only in the market for a car ride, not any other type.

Thankfully, it was all totally innocent. Zara was the taxi driver's daughter who was perfecting her English in the hope of moving to London to get a job. This was a perfect opportunity for her to practice and act as interpreter for the trip.

Zara was 21, with long black hair and was of slim build. She reminded me of an attractive Greek girl of the type that work in shops in Glyfada or Kolonaiki.

She spent most of the journey talking to us. Strangely, she wore sunglasses with one lens missing. I figured that she must be unable to afford a new pair, whilst she must have concluded that one shaded eye was better than none at all.

This reminded me of an experience in India a decade prior. I was on a small group holiday where we all got on extremely well apart from an oddball character who we christened Walter, as he reminded us of the soppy comic-book character who was victimised by Denis the Menace in the 'Beano'.

Walter and I had decided to buy some cheap prescription glasses. I was after some sunglasses whilst he wanted some sunglasses and a standard clear pair.

We chose our frames, advised our prescription and arranged to come back next day to collect. Bizarrely Walter had chosen the same frame for both of his pairs of glasses.

Something was lost in translation as when we picked them up, Walter was presented with a single pair with one dark lens and one clear lens! I 'pissed myself' with laughter and couldn't wait to tell the rest of the group. For some reason Walter would not let me take a picture of him wearing his unusual fashion statement!

Back to '07 and Hamish nearly pissed himself at the border control point. Not through laughter, but through drinking excessive water in the heat of the day.

Here we were, stuck in no man's land behind a queue of cars. On the 'pissometer' scale from one-ten he was fluctuating between nine & ten, pretty desperate stuff.

As he squirmed in the back seat, we slowly but surely crept to the front. The disinterested border guards nonchalantly waved at our passports to confirm acceptance, however Zara's dad's paperwork required ten minutes of scrutiny before we were allowed to continue.

Hamish was now firmly stuck on ten and close to losing it. Relief was at hand in a rundown café on the other side. He did not care about the flies or stink as he experienced almost orgasmic relief. I quite enjoyed my tea too!

Chapter Five – The Former Yugoslavia

We were dropped off at Bar's well-kept station, looking resplendent with its freshly swept platforms, shiny black steam locomotive proudly on display (a common sight in many Eastern European stations) and plenty of pretty flowers in tubs & boxes.

The setting was also very pleasant with the region's famous mountains looming around us as far as the eye could see (Montenegro = Black Mountain).

We wished Zara luck with her dream of moving to London and het father a safe journey back home.

There were a couple of hours to kill before the train to Podgorica. With the station on the distant periphery of anything in particular, we were left with the single option of a small bar/restaurant just outside the station entrance.

This was also very neat & tidy with plenty of interesting adornments hanging from every available space. Furthermore, they had our absolute favourite DB, the quite superb Nikšićko.

This was the local brew that we first had the pleasure of sampling during our visit to Niš the previous year.

Montenegro (Europe's newest country at the time thanks to their reportedly amicable separation from Serbia in 2006) was making a very good early impression. Furthermore, they had adopted the Euro as their national currency, so no confusing beans to contend with.

Bar to Podgorica Departure 14.05 Arrival 15.01, 56KM

A fabulous DB and a cheese salad baguette later, all was well with the world. We were certainly ready for the journey, with the train trip from Bar to the capital described as very pleasant, skirting past lake and mountain.

And so it proved, with Hamish and I on permanent picture alert.

Wills

Despite the very impressive scenery, the journey was most memorable to me for the battle of wills between Hamish and a local man.

The chap in his thirties insisted on smoking, despite the clear no smoking signs. Hamish huffed and puffed for a while, before deciding to take decisive action to alleviate his suffering sinuses.

Nothing as bold as asking the rough-looking stranger to refrain from smoking, but in an obvious display of displeasure he forcibly opened the window.

I half hoped that it would be one of those embarrassing occasions for Hamish where you struggle to open the window with any panache and are then caught in the dilemma of using a little more force to prise it open, trying to work out the complex opening mechanism in a few seconds flat or giving up gracefully and returning red-faced to your seat.

Hats off to him though, he had worked out the system before pouncing and opened it with aplomb.

Although the weather was pleasant enough, Hamish's action did lead to the carriage getting noticeably cooler, so the air polluter soon slammed the window shut again with as much ceremony as Hamish had demonstrated in opening it.

This left my mate fuming and when the bloke started his own fumes again, Hamish decided to strike once more.

The carriage became cooler once more, so as before the perpetrator of the smoke repeated his retort.

This happened for a third time, each time the displeasure of the combatants becoming more and more audible.

Then at last, just as I was imagining bailing Hamish out of Montenegrin jail for affray, a moral victory was won. The ticket inspector arrived and saw what was going on.

He helpfully admonished the smoker, who then left the train at the next stop. We were not sure whether this was voluntary or not, but we were able to continue the journey in smoke-free warmth and Hamish was able to claim a victory for the non-smoker!

Back to the scenery outside, it was indeed very beautiful. The shimmering blue lake that went on for several miles was particularly pleasingly picturesque.

It was home to a plethora of birdlife, a multitude of grasses of many different shapes & hues, and dozens of people traversing the calm waters either for pleasure or profession.

Our arrival at Podgorica would mean we alighted a train for the final time on this trip; it was to be buses from now on sadly. First stop Kotor, situated on the Balkan's largest fjord.

Hamish has the in-built ability to choose the correct side of the bus to travel on. The side where there will be no annoying sun in your eyes or the side that will give you the best scenery during the journey.

This is probably really straightforward to most people, but I do not have a clue how you work it out. Pot luck it is for me, with about a 50/50 success rate.

Hamish hit the jackpot again, a nice shady journey hugging the coast with a window view out into the deep blue yonder.

This was one of those rare fabulous bus rides, as we cut through the mountains and down to the coastal waters of the Adriatic. Budvar especially looked lovely sat by the sea with its terracotta roofs glinting in the late afternoon sun.

We soon arrived in Kotor, a medieval walled town with a castle high above. It was a lovely tranquil place. We stayed two nights and apart from an energising yomp up to the castle on day one, it was time to relax.

Hell Hole

We delayed said yomp until the sun had passed its hottest point, so as to stay relatively comfortable for the steep ascent

Up at the fortifications Hamish and I witnessed what we both agreed was potentially the worst accident waiting to happen that you could possibly imagine.

A crater in the ground led to a twenty-foot drop. Hazardous enough, however this hole had a coup de grace. Growing out of its perimeter was a large shrub bedecked in yellow flowers, catnip to hordes of wasps, hornets, bees and unidentified red-winged beasties.

To trip and fall down this hell hole would likely see you taking a large portion of shrub with you, of course accompanied by an angry mob dressed predominantly in black and yellow.

The thought of lying at the bottom of the pit, legs buckled, with all those winged guests for company made us both shudder. Dante's Inferno, Pandora's Box and Room 101 all rolled into one!

We bravely teetered over the edge for a photo of the nest of vipers and shuddered once more. It would have been hell on earth if either of us had lost our balance and crashed through the seething throng - in our biased opinions only of course!

"I will give you a pound if you take a run up and jump across the crater wearing only your underpants," I suggested to Hamish.

Moving swiftly on...

The view from the top of the hill was marvelous, with the bright blue fjord stretching away to our left and around the mountain-flanked bend.

A riverboat bobbed gently on its moorings and as far as the eye could see, terracotta roofs stood proudly, interspersed with plenty of greenery. This really was a lovely place to live it seemed.

Back downhill after a very pleasant stroll amongst the ruins, the old town was equally lovely and with a great choice of restaurants and cafés in which to refresh our parts. We also took in England's aforementioned hugely important Euro 2008 qualifier in Russia.

Sitting in a picturesque square, drinking DB on a warm pleasant evening whilst watching football and all seemed well with the world. When Wayne Rooney put England ahead in Moscow, the portents were even rosier.

It didn't last though. England lost 2-1 and eventually bowed out of the competition finishing behind Croatia and that day's hosts in the qualifying group - some of you may remember the 'wally with the brolly' (soon to be ex-manager Steve McLaren) at rain-soaked Wembley as elimination was secured against the Croats.

Never mind, another DB and pizza soon erased the bad taste. "I will give you a pound if you buy one of those marionettes and then set yourself up as a street entertainer on the corner of the square," I challenged Hamish. We made do with photos of the large colourful puppets for sale instead.

Kotor is another one of the lovely European destinations that I have vowed to take the good wife to in the future. Like Krakow and Istanbul, we are yet to make it together, but they do remain 'on the ever-expanding list.'

Au Revoir Black Mountains

Next day it was a bus again - this time along the coast to Dubrovnik.

This was another lovely road journey as we followed the fjord inland and out again to the coast.

We soon approached Dubrovnik on the road high above, to be met with a stunning birds eye view of the ancient walled town, the marina and a huge cruise ship that was moored up.

The enormous vessel looked majestic with the white cables of a suspension bridge behind it. A great mental picture that would need following up with a digital version before we left.

We were staying out of the Old Town in a package style hotel in Lapad, twenty-minutes' walk from the main sights. Intriguingly there was a world under-eighteens ladies tennis tournament going on virtually next door to the hotel.

Naturally Hamish and I decided to watch for a few minutes (hours!) for purely sporting reasons. These could be tomorrow's champions after all and we wanted to say "we were there" when the new Monica Seles was unveiled.

We were treated to some marathon rallies, lots of grunting and a few ponytail swinging, racket bashing, tantrums.

We also viewed at close quarters where the girls put their spare balls when serving. A revealing insight into ladies' tennis all round!

Today was Saturday, so we decided to walk to the coastal part of Lapad, to keep tabs on the afternoon's English football unfold on our mobile phones whilst listening to the relaxing sounds of the Adriatic waves.

My main City team were not playing that afternoon but Exeter City and West Ham won to leave us both happy and in need of a beer to celebrate. No DB but blonde was welcome all the same with its accompanying nuts and pretzels.

Clean Old Town

That evening we explored the Old Town. It was largely devoid of tourists - we figured the busy season had finished. The town was built in similar (but much larger) fashion to Kotor.

Romantic poet Lord Byron described the walled city as 'the pearl of the Adriatic', and with good reason. The magnificent curtain of walls surrounding the marble streets and baroque buildings were all lit up atmospherically.

We walked along the three-hundred-metre-long main pedestrian thoroughfare called Placa, with its mélange of cafés and tourist shops.

We had entered through the western entrance called the Pile Gate. The first striking structure we came across was the 15th-century Large Onofrio's Fountain (Small Onofrio's Fountain was at the east end).

We passed the imposing Dubrovnik Bell Tower and walked the length of the enthralling street to the bell tower attached to the Franciscan monastery also at the east end. This building housed the museum chronicling the '90s conflict.

Much of Dubrovnik was badly damaged in the war as the port city was incessantly shelled by the Serbs and although the city has since been repaired to its former glory, it became clear that the conflict will never be forgotten as indelible scars remain in people's memories, if not so much on the buildings.

I remembered seeing the shells and bullets raining down on the Jewell of the Adriatic when it was shown on British TV news reports.

Dubrovnik was just becoming a popular UK tourist destination until the war started and it was viewed by us Brits as a great shame that the Serbs were picking on the beautiful buildings not for military reasons, but to crush the Croatian morale at seeing their prized asset reduced to rubble.

Croatia had in fact demilitarised the region purely for the reason of protecting their pride and joy - suffice to say that the Serbian tactics were widely criticised.

The repair work had been completed expertly - only some slightly brighter tiles or stone here and there gave the game away.

Most of the restaurants were of the Italian variety, so pasta and red wine was the order of the evening and very nice too.

It was also time for me to direct a conundrum at my pal. "Hamish, can you think of a genuine grammatically correct sentence where the word 'and' appears five times consecutively?"

Naturally he could not, and in fairness it took me several attempts to remember the answer. Here goes.

'A man owns a pub called the Coach and Horses. He decides he needs a new pub sign, so he employs the services of a sign writer to produce a new design.

The sign-writer sketches out a new sign with predictably a picture of a stage coach and two black horses with the words 'The Coach and Horses' inscribed below.

He asks the landlord's opinion to which he replied, "I love the design, but could we have a slightly bigger gap between Coach and and and and and Horses?"

This of course led to the story of the Caribbean cup game where both teams had it in their own best interests to score an own goal. I will let you stew on the reasons for that one for a while, whilst I carry on with the rest of the chapter.

Daytime Dalliance

Everybody who I knew that had been to Dubrovnik had told me that a highlight of the visit was to walk the city walls - they were not wrong.

This gave the pleasurable double whammy of a fabulous perspective of the ancient town and also great views of the sparkling blue waters of the Adriatic.

We started early and walked the whole circumference of the Old Town in about two hours - it was well worth it, the views being as fantastic as described in giving a bird's eye view of everything.

As we alighted at 11.30, we realised we had timed it perfectly as there were now horrendous queues of tourists forming, keen to see if their own friends had been right to talk so enthusiastically of the tour of the walls.

We had seen the reason for this from atop the walls. Two large cruise ships carrying an estimated combined five thousand passengers had docked.

Most of the mass of passengers had disembarked into the Old Town. Scores of tour groups snaked behind their leaders, eager to take in the sights and historical information being imparted.

Balls II

Dubrovnik was transformed from a peaceful, crowd-free pleasure into a seething, squirming throng. Sit down lunch or drink? Forget it, standing room only. After a crowded look at the wonderful Assumption Cathedral, we decided to head back to Lapad for our refreshment and to take in more of the tennis.

In an unexpected twist, one of the coaches noticed our intense appreciation of the tennis and came over to speak with us - there were hardly any spectators after all for this most minor of championships.

"You like tennis I see. Do you play?" Occasionally I replied. The last time had been a decade or more ago and even then, I wasn't that good. Hamish on the other hand was a little better than me, not that this indicated any real prowess on his part.

In an act of devilment, I then announced that Hamish was a pretty good player.

No sooner had the words passed my lips than the Croatian tennis professional turned to Hamish and asked if he fancied a knock up.

Hamish, not sure whether to refute my claims or to politely decline, instead maintained my credibility, foolishly dropping himself in it by merely stating that he had not played for a while and was a bit rusty.

The Croatian then insisted and stated that he just needed a warm up against a male opponent as he had an over fifties tournament starting next day - he would not be on full power and just needed someone to hit a few balls with.

Hamish was now a little flustered, far too disorientated to make up a plausible excuse such as a knee injury or bad back, instead feebly asserting that he had no training shoes.

"Fear not, I have plenty, you are size forty-one or forty-two I think, please wait here," came the response that Hamish did not want to hear.

When he was out of earshot, my pal turned to me and questioned my parentage!

I was in hysterics, not quite believing that my remark had got us to this unexpected stage. I was laughing too hard (not to mention being disinclined) to offer a way out of the predicament and had to step on my foot to stop the mirth as the proposed opponent returned.

The trainers fitted like a glove and as Hamish was already in shorts and t-shirt, he was ready to go. Vedrun handed him one of his spare rackets and off they went to one of the practice courts.

I could not believe that Hamish was going through with it. I now faced an almighty dilemma.

I had left my camera back at the hotel after our walls experience, but I figured that the knock up would be over in a few moments and if I went to get it, I would miss the whole hilarious spectacle.

Sod it; this would have to be a memory of the mind rather than a photographic souvenir.

Give Hamish his due; he did look the part as he went through his stretches, mirroring Vedrun's lead perfectly. That was where the illusion ended however!

Vedrun knocked a gentle shot in the direction of the awkward Englishman, who hit his return into the bottom of the net.

The next 'dolly drop' was returned skywards off the edge of the loaned racket, eventually the ball bouncing just a few feet away from where he had connected.

I was now beside myself; this was ranking as one of the funniest spectacles of my life.

The seemingly exasperated Croat then sent a gentle lob in Hamish's direction. This time he connected with full power sending the ball sailing right out of court!

Hamish's agony was about to end. Not however, before a number of the female tennis players had cottoned onto what was going on. They too were laughing at the entertainment that lay before them. This was absolutely priceless.

Vedrun called to Hamish that he was going to try a serve. I (and Hamish by the look of trepidation on his face) was expecting a howitzer to speed past my friend's large ears. In the event, Vedrun served a viciously spinning slow serve, which Hamish stupidly thought he could get to.

As the ball spun back on him tying him in knots, he slipped on the synthetic surface and grazed his knee, drawing blood. That was to be his last act, Vedrun deciding that he had had enough 'practice'.

As the girls and his travel buddy grinned widely, Hamish was to be spared any further humiliation, thanking his tormentor for the 'game'.

As I skipped and Hamish limped back to the hotel, I theorised that the whole incident had been done on purpose. The girls had noticed our close attentions and had plotted revenge, setting up the coach to take one of us on.

Just a theory, but I found it hard to explain why an obvious professional (albeit a middle-aged one) would ask a stranger and amateur for a knock up.

Hamish just blamed me for the whole episode - it took a few beers for him to see the funny side.

As I mentioned this had been one of the funniest things that I had ever witnessed and one equally as amusing had happened in the past that incredibly also featured Hamish and tennis.

The previous comedic episode took place in a Bulgarian beach resort in the mid '90's. We had travelled as a three together with our mutual pal Lang and met three Norwegian guys who we hung out with.

We decided that a game of tennis doubles would be a good way to pass a couple of hours. The teams were set as Norway v England, on a rotational basis.

At three games all, it was Hamish's turn to serve. At 15-30 and poised to send over one of his looping serves, he suddenly started thrashing his arms around wildly and set off on a mazy run around the tramlines of the court.

We soon realised why as it became apparent that he was being pursued by a couple of dozen alarmingly angry Bulgarian hornets, buzzing loudly and lined up in attack formation. Stupidly he dispensed with his racket in his utter panic, the one useful weapon that he had at his disposal to swat the wretched beasts.

We were bent double with laughter at this sight, but soon had to straighten up as he led the by now furious flying felons in our direction.

'Ping', the first hornet was dispatched with ease and now sat motionless between the strings of my racket.

'Thwack', Dag did the business with two in one swipe to get Norway one up on the hornet slaying scoreboard.

Owwwwwwww! Hamish took a revenge sting on the ankle before managing to stamp the critter to death. Technically 2-2, but a point should probably have been deducted for taking a hit against.

We eventually lost count as three whirling rackets managed to wipe out the yellow & black squadron.

At this point we noticed the grubby Bulgarian gardener in hysterics. It was his tree clipping that had disturbed the winged stingers. He had however got off scot-free and instead had been treated to five minutes of mirthful mayhem.

As peace was restored in court, he described the scene in his basic English as, "most funniest thing I ever see."

That was the end of the match. Hamish retired hurt (wounded pride, dignity & ankle), whilst the rest of us needed a beer to wind down from all that adrenalin and begin a stint of relentless piss taking for the next few hours.

This current trip was to be a real sporting one. The night of the latest tennis related merriment at Hamish's expense happened to be the Rugby Union World Cup Final played at the Stade de France in Paris.

England had of course made it there against all expectations and were considered big underdogs against a South African XV who had soundly thrashed the Red Rose country in the group stages.

I bolted a pizza and left Hamish to enjoy a more leisurely evening whilst I dashed to an Irish bar for the game.

This would in fact be the second successive final for England, both of which I witnessed whilst abroad. In 2003 I had been in Johannesburg and watched England's nail-biting victory against the Australian Wallabies Down Under on TV in a hotel bar.

It had been an incredible experience; a fantastic victory followed by me then being heartily congratulated by scores of Springboks, happy that England had defeated their Southern Hemisphere rivals.

This occasion was somewhat different. The bar was so packed that I could forget any notion of having a drink and the match itself was a huge disappointment. Not only did England lose 15-6, but also the match itself never really got going, not even producing a try.

There was one moment of high drama when England's Mark Cueto had a try disallowed for stepping into touch. The margin was so narrow to have been invisible to the naked eye, taking much scrutiny of the video evidence before the referee finally ruled 'no try'.

So, after a few minutes of mayhem as the largely English viewers in the bar had been convinced like me of a legitimate score that would have put England in with a great chance, was to quickly subside into groans of disappointment. Not what I had dreamt of.

I dejectedly re-joined my mate, ordered another bottle of red and drowned my sorrows.

Day Trippers

I awoke next day with a sore head and dry mouth, but with no time for a hangover lie-in as Sunday was our last full day of the trip, a day for activity and a toss-up between going to the Croatian island of Hvar and taking the bus to Mostar. The famous Bosnian town had won out.

We had checked the bus timetable and there was one leaving at nine and returning at six so we would have a good five to six hours to explore.

The 07.30 alarm could be ignored no longer, in any case my travel companion dropping an odorous calling card made the haven of the bathroom an appealing place to be.

I was not exactly looking forward to the journey ahead as we sloped off to the bus station, 15-minutes' walk away.

We (Hamish actually made the transaction as I was not yet up to speech) secured tickets for the departure, but were not able to buy a return, the helpful lady explaining that we needed to purchase this in Mostar.

The journey lasted around three hours and although picturesque in places was largely not noteworthy – in truth I slept for most of it.

Most excitement was provoked when we crossed a railway line.

We must travel on that line one day we agreed. TC later confirmed it to be the Ploče to Sarajevo line, which indeed we were to traverse a few years later.

Arriving at midday, we went to buy our return tickets as advised. Not quite as we had planned though - the winter timetable had kicked in that weekend and the last bus back was thirty minutes hence!

We were faced with either a journey for journey's sake or taking a chance on finding an alternative means back. We chose the latter, figuring that we could afford a taxi later.

That was something for worrying about at some time in the future as now we had to explore and witness Mostar's famous bridge that had been completely demolished during the Yugoslav conflict and rebuilt in its original state a few years prior to our visit.

The bridge over the Neretva River was the link between the Christian side and the Muslim side, with its mosques and hammam. The Croat military forces had smashed it on 9th November 1993 to symbolically cut off the Muslims and hurt their morale during the Croat-Bosniak conflict.

The rebuilt bridge looked fantastic. Bright honey-yellow stone spanning beautiful blue waters below. Much of the stone was in fact from the original structure, lovingly fitted back together piece by piece.

There was a further attraction too. Brave young members of Mostar's diving club took to diving off the bridge into the relatively shallow waters twenty-four metres below.

We watched the spectacle for the first time from the bridge. A group of young men started by collecting money from the tourists. Once they had garnered sufficient, it was time. One of their number peeled off his shirt and climbed up onto the bridge ramparts.

He then encouraged the watching crowd to clap by clapping his own hands high above his head, before he sprung upwards and came down in a vertical position rather than a bona fide dive. The build-up had lasted a good half an hour and the spectacle was over in seconds. Well worth the wait though.

We witnessed two more 'dives' from the riverbank – a fantastic position from which to view the whole of the graceful plunge, immaculate entry and spluttering resurface.

The rest of our time in the peaceful town was spent leisurely ambling around the myriad of craft shops, climbing to the top of the main mosque minaret and eating Arabic food (particularly hummus, my absolute favourite) in a riverside restaurant just down from the bridge.

One shop in particular was owned or managed by a stunningly beautiful girl. Suddenly two guys with little interest in purchasing gifts up to that point, were now browsing intently.

Hamish bought a sequined pouch for his mobile phone, just for the sake of it! It took him ages to find the correct money and then he took to asking for directions to several points of apparent interest.

A simple transaction therefore took at least fifteen minutes, with the Bosnian Beauty seemingly oblivious to the blatant delaying tactics. Whatever the case, she politely answered all of the direction questions put to her, the answers to which neither of us really listened to and certainly had no intention of following.

By chance we stumbled across the central cemetery – row upon row of identical graves like something out of the Somme or Ypres. The dates this time mainly put death at 1993 (around eighty years since the WWI tragedies), the majority of casualties falling at the time of the Croat siege. Time for several minutes' introspection about the follies of war, but we were soon back to relaxed strolling.

Carpeted

As I mentioned, the place was now peaceful and also seemingly very laid back. One incident however threatened to shatter the illusion! Let me explain.

The travel and photography magazines always say that you should ask permission before taking somebody's photo.

That way, not only will you avoid offending your intended model, but you will get a better shot with a full expression, as opposed to the rushed surreptitious version showing half a face masked by shadows.

This advice is of course sound, but there are times that you just can't be bothered to ask, especially with older subjects who may not understand you.

Whilst walking amongst the shops that line the riverbanks near Mostar's bridge, I spied a character that I just had to capture.

The old man's walnut lined face told a thousand stories of conflicts, hardships and a life lived to the full.

Wild white hair, pointed snowy beard, white cotton tunic & trouser ensemble covering his meagre body, topped with a white fez shaped hat with gold braiding. He made a striking subject.

He carried a red carpet over his shoulder that looked heavier than he was, but moved at purposeful speed.

I wondered whether he was late for a fitting or perhaps he was off to sell his wares to a tourist, who would surely expect a photo as part of the transaction.

Such was his speed and agility over the uneven surface that a photo would be tricky, even with a powerful zoom. What the heck - go on sports mode and click away, easy to delete the bad ones later.

Suddenly Catweazle, as I had named him after the '70s UK TV character played by Geoffrey Bayldon, stopped and changed direction. As I viewed him through my lens, I eventually realised when he was but a few yards away from me that he was shouting and the shouts were aimed at me.

I was stunned when the carpet swished in my direction and clipped me on the side of my head, sending my sunglasses to the floor and me down on one knee.

If looks could kill, I would not be here to write this now. Expecting a volley of abuse, Mr. Weazle simply turned on his heels with a satisfied smirk but without a further word, and headed back to wherever he had been going in the first place.

The divers were no longer the top spectacle in town - it was now me! Quite a crowd had gathered to see what the commotion was all about. Tourists looked on open-mouthed and wide-eyed, whilst locals grinned knowingly.

Hamish was in stitches once more (after he checked I wasn't hurt of course!), whilst I just wanted to slip away as quickly as possible, both my right knee and my ego bearing the bruises of the incident.

Carpeted by a pensioner, whatever next!

Hamish reckoned the guy was a descendant of Sinbad and was now off to find a flat piece of land to launch his magic carpet.

He had certainly sinned badly as far as I was concerned and I was not in the mood to issue a pardon!

I needed a beer to help me recover. Time to find a bar with one proviso - no carpets!

After the recovery beer and what had been a fantastic six hours at the wonderful place (carpet man excepted), it was time to secure our transport home.

The Party's Over

A deal was struck with a taxi driver - €70 to take us to our hotel door. A tad more expensive than the bus, but worth every cent due to the fabulous few hours we had spent in Mostar.

The journey back took us right through the Bosnian-Serb territory of Republika Srpska, the other political entity of the country alongside Bosnia and Herzegovina.

The creation of the modern Republika Srpska in 1991 was formed from six Serb Autonomous Regions during the Yugoslav Wars. It became an internationally recognised territory within the state of Bosnia and Herzegovina in 1995 following the end of those particular conflicts.

Srpska maintains its own parliamentary system and a free economy similar to the rest of the country. It has its de facto capital in Banja Luka, the second largest city of Bosnia Herzegovina with a population just under 200,000.

As you would no doubt think, this is a fractious arrangement. Srpska has its own Independence Day on 9th January, whilst its neighbour to the west celebrates the official Bosnian Independence Day on 1st March. There have also been representations made from Banja Luka that Srpska should become fully autonomous and a member of the United Nations in its own right.

On our journey home from Mostar, it soon descended into darkness and at one stage we drove through a complete wilderness akin to Dartmoor's bleakest parts.

This coincided with Hamish reaching breaking point in his need for bladder relief. The taxi driver spoke little or no English and I witnessed the comical sight and sound of Hamish explaining he needed the loo.

He chose the action and sound of pulling a chain and flushing the toilet. Thankfully that was understood and he didn't need to resort to pointing to his nether regions, as lord knows where that would have got us!

We pulled over and Hamish clambered out of the passenger seat for a roadside pee. Hilariously the taxi driver did the same and despite all the acres of space available, he stood right next to Hamish like they were in neighbouring urinals!

Quick as a flash I took a rear-side photo of the two united in relief. The result may have been two murky shadows in the gloom, but I know exactly what the picture represents and it makes me laugh every time I look at it.

We were kept waiting for around twenty minutes at the border control - there seemed to be some sort of heated debate going on, before we were finally waved through and dropped at our hotel around nine.

Next day was homeward day. The hotel had a distinct end of season air about it and we saw absolutely no other guests. After settling up we were shown the door, which was promptly locked behind us. We then saw the handwritten sign hanging in one of the glass panes - 'we re-open 14th April 2008'.

There were a couple of hours to kill before we had to go to the airport and as luck would have it, the final of the tennis tournament was being played.

And the winner was…………Natasa Zorić of Serbia. No, I have never heard of her either - not surprising, as her world rank as at the end of 2011 was 797.

You may remember that I mentioned a Caribbean football conundrum. Well this is what happened.

It concerned an international match in January 1994 between Barbados and Grenada.

The game was part of the qualification round for the 1994 Caribbean Cup. Due to an unusual scoring rule, it was alternately in Barbados's then Grenada's best interest to score an own goal.

The organisers of the tournament imposed a rule requiring all matches to have a winner and had chosen an unusual variant of the golden goal rule, which meant that the first goal scored in extra-time not only won the match, but also counted as double.

Barbados started the match needing to win by a margin of at least two goals to qualify for the final tournament. With Barbados winning two nil, Grenada pulled one back with seven minutes remaining.

A 2-1 win for Barbados, would have taken Grenada through on goal difference. The Bajans initially tried to score a legitimate third goal to take them through, but with time running out, they realised that their best bet was to score an own goal, to take the match into extra-time where a solitary goal scored by them would take them through 4-2 due to that 'golden goal counts as double' rule.

One of the Barbados strikers scored the required own goal in collusion with his goalkeeper to make it 2-2.

The initially stunned Grenadines, now realised that it would be in their own best interests to also score an own goal in the few minutes that remained of the regulation ninety as a 3-2 loss would take them through.

This led to the bizarre sight of twenty-one players in Grenada's penalty area in the dying seconds, Barbados desperately trying to stop their opponents scoring a goal in *their own net (only the Barbados goalie stayed back in case of a Grenada breakaway attempt).*

The Bajans were literally lined up on their opponent's goal line, not to try and score a goal, but to try and prevent one.

Try as the might, Grenada could not force the ball 'home', with the game finishing 2-2 and heading to extra-time where the first goal scored would give the scoring team a 4-2 victory.

The skullduggery paid off for Barbados, with them scoring four minutes into the extra-time period for that 4-2 victory that took them through at Grenada's expense.

Bizarre but true - the rule was promptly scrapped for following tournaments!

Chapter Six - Old Town Rules
(September 2012)

We took the late afternoon flight to the Croatian capital of Zagreb in late September 2012, arriving at our budget hotel just before nine-thirty.

The itinerary this time would see us take in three former Yugoslav countries, before finishing in Bulgaria. Preparation had followed the last minute.com approach of recent years, but all seemed to come together in the end. No new countries, but plenty of fresh experiences were planned.

Our spartan accommodation was thirty-plus minute walk from the centre but handily placed for the tram, so we wasted no time in heading in that direction.

It was on the tram that I discovered my new phone wouldn't allow me to roam. Blast! I would need to sort that out.

We got out at the floodlit central square, and a nice one it was too with its Baroque buildings and cobbled surface. It was pedestrianised, aside from the trams, and housed the tourist information office we noted.

We were both Hank Marvin (starving) so went off in search of a restaurant. I am ashamed to say we ended up in McDonald's, as we couldn't locate anywhere else.

We were to discover the next day that we had only needed to climb some steps from the main square to be in a street crammed with independent bars and restaurants, but it was too late and we were too tired and hungry to explore just yet.

Next door to the burger joint stood a small bar that served a very nice DB, one of which finished our first evening very well.

It was also here that I discovered Wi-Fi on my mobile meaning that I could surf and email for free from establishments that offered a connection. Eureka!!

OK, I admit I was terribly slow on the uptake, but had only recently purchased my first ever smart phone.

Morning Has Broken

This was a new city for us, and we were keen for an early start to explore. First, we had to secure our overnight train berths to Split for the next day, so we walked the mile or so to the train station with the aim to do just that.

Transaction duly completed satisfactorily, we were now free to roam and discover what the city had to offer.

From the station it was a short stroll into the heart of the city. We both very soon started to love the place. It had a chilled vibe and some great architecture. Trams zoomed about the place, but walkers seemed in no particular hurry to get anywhere.

We took in the main cathedral and opera house (booking Carmen for that night), before heading to the main square (named Ban Jelacic Square) that we had visited briefly the night before.

It really was a fine square with a church in one corner and several statues including the main one of acclaimed general Count Josip

Jelacic on his horse.

It was also a focal meeting point with many small groups of friends just chilling and chatting.

Climbing up that small flight of steps we came to the Old Town. First port of call was a bustling and colourful flower market where we lingered for a few shots, before continuing down a short restaurant lined hill and into the oldest part of town proper.

More cobbled streets, interesting gift shops, medieval walls and small picturesque squares with multi-coloured buildings. It was fabulous to just meander through the small streets and discover what lay around the corner.

Our map indicated that there was a long pedestrian street nearby, so we made for it. It was home to what must have been around sixty cafés, bars and restaurants. Stuff McDonald's we thought in unison.

It was time for a DB, some fried potatoes with sour cream and a chill-out. I had recently become a convert to Facebook and Twitter and was enjoying the experience.

I had resisted this for a long time but finally took the plunge to help promote my first book that was to be published shortly thereafter ('This is How it Feels to be City', a book chronicling the lows, highs & honour of what it meant to support Manchester City for forty odd years).

I therefore caught up on my social media while Hamish read the LP pages. This was a great way to have an effective conversation with Mrs Wilbur without costing a penny. I really was a convert.

It was now five in the afternoon, so we headed back to change for the showing of Bizet's masterpiece of unrequited love. As we had just started the trip our clothes still looked OK, so we did not stand out too much from the smart crowd.

The opera house was the usual affair of ornate stucco ceiling, grand chandeliers, plum red velvet seats and circular gilded auditorium.

Carmen did not disappoint - Don Juan still failed to win the heart of the Seville cigarette seller who gives the opera its name. The music was as wonderful as ever.

Groundhog Day

Zagreb was fairly compact, and we had seen most of the sights on day one. After wandering around and retracing many of our steps from the previous day, we were done. There were still seven hours to go until our overnight train, so what to do?

I suggested the cinema, and this is what we decided to do. The tourist information centre pointed us in the right direction and a ten-minute tram ride took us right there.

Upon scanning the 'now showing' list we had two options - Madagascar 4 and Resident Evil in 3D. I didn't want the animated feature and surprisingly Hamish approved the latter film. We had no idea what it was about, no idea if it was a sequel, prequel or original and only knew Milla Jovovich of the stars appearing in it.

So, we put on our dark glasses not knowing what to expect. It turned out to be an enjoyable romp if not always easy to follow.

There were quite a few twists and turns and duplications of characters, so predictably Hamish did not understand the story.

However, we had both enjoyed it in our own way and felt refreshed after all that day's walking. Furthermore, we were down to four hours until departure time.

We therefore had time to enjoy a good meal and two DBs each. After that we went to purchase two take away DBs each from the bar next door to McD's, as theirs (Velebitsko) was the best we had tasted in Zagreb. The barman helpfully warned that we faced arrest if we drank in the street!

Two trams later we arrived at the station via the hotel and clambered aboard, having first waited for a party of four immaculately dressed Italians and their twelve items of designer luggage to struggle onto our carriage, losing much of their suave demeanour in the process.

Zagreb to Split, Departure 23.20 Arrival 08.10, 435 KM

We cracked open the DB in our two-bed private compartment. However, we were so bushed from the long day and beers we had already consumed, that we barely managed two gulps before we gave in to the tiredness, foregoing the traditional drunken conversation.

I had the best train night's sleep ever, no doubt thanks to exhaustion and inebriation combined with the gentle nine-hour amble to do just over four hundred kilometres.

Coastal Waters

We arrived in beautiful early morning sunshine. The train station was right on the harbour front, so we decided to sit in one of the many waterside cafés for a coffee and croissant pick up before the task of locating our central hotel.

It was so pleasant and relaxing that a second coffee followed. Our extended rest had absolutely nothing to do with the trio of very attractive girls who sat opposite us!

We could delay no longer and hoisted our rucksacks to our shoulders (Hamish using a chair as a prop as was the norm), before following the harbour wall to the 'city' centre.

Split's walled Old Town is almost entirely constructed of light stone and its paved streets are a labyrinth of narrow alleys opening out into large leafy squares.

Even famed explorer Sir Ranulph Fiennes would have had difficulty discovering the correct alley that led to our hotel, so Hamish decided to pop into a local shop to ask directions.

He reappeared only moments later, scowling and muttering "bitch," under his breath.

The unfriendly vendor had pointed out in no uncertain terms that she wasn't tourist information and bade him a far from fond farewell.

We later discussed a Pretty Woman type revenge - buy loads of the same kind of tat that she was selling at a different location, walk into her shop laden down by rival shop's bags, loudly mention that the nice shopkeeper who we purchased the goods from had been most helpful with directions and then leave, lesson delivered.

Even a OPD was not sufficient to tempt either of us to do it for real, but the thought was a good one.

Undaunted, Hamish changed some euros and got directions from the exchange clerk - we were actually own a weakling's stone's throw away.

Our room wasn't ready, but the laid-back reception dude gave us info aplenty, a decent map and the hotel rules (none to speak of except "if you bring girls back, please be quiet!").

When he asked if we needed anything else just to ask, I did ponder asking him to run a manners workshop for tat sellers, but again this was a fleeting fancy.

Leaving our rucksacks, we went for a wander around the pretty harbour with its ferries bound for the Croatian islands of Brac & Hvar, plus further afield to Ancona in Italy.

In the shadow of the ferries, sail boats and dinghies bobbed gently on their moorings, all overlooked by Split's two most distinctive structures - its striking cathedral jostling for skyline with the many other buildings built up the hillside, and the iconic clock tower with its bright blue clock face smiling down on those below.

At a pit stop, Hamish looked closely at the map and announced that there was a pleasant circular walk around the headland. I agreed we should do it and off we set. If he had mentioned that it was fourteen kilometres in the afternoon heat, I may have thought twice!

Luckily, we had enough water for the hike, whilst the little packs of raisins that Mrs Wilbur had so thoughtfully packed were extremely welcome for energy kicks.

The walk was well worth it, starting through a pine forest and soon following the craggy coastline. For the first half there was very little sign of life apart from the odd vehicle, but once we turned the tip of the headland, sporadic huge dwellings became apparent, tucked neatly on the slopes above the road.

These were Beverley Hills like - tennis courts, swimming pools, olive groves, enormous patios etc. We speculated as to the Croatian owners – famed tennis champion Goran Ivanisović or ex-manager of the national football team Slavan Bilić perhaps, or maybe even an ex-Communist power broker?

For the duration of the walk crickets chirped wildly. I recounted a story when I had been in Greece and ordered a dish of crickets!

I had wanted tzatziki (the yoghurt and cucumber dip) to accompany my calamari and not tizikia (crickets)! Fond as I am of most things from South East Asia, this does not extend to eating creepy crawlies. At least I gave my wife and the waiter a good laugh.

Two thirds into the energy-sapping walk, we noticed a flotilla of sailing boats in the distance out to sea. A klaxon blasted and they were off, splitting into two groups of fifteen or so, resembling demented swans-a-swimming and jockeying for position.

With the London Olympics still fresh in the memory, I wondered whether quadruple gold medalist Ben Ainslie was taking part, the only sailing sportsman at my immediate recall. Probably not, he was more likely to be on a luxury yacht somewhere after all of his exploits.

As we neared the final stretch, the jagged cliff face and rock-strewn waters gave way to sandy beaches sprinkled with sun worshippers. It was still bloody hot at four; thanks for the weight loss programme Hamish!

We were now in the marina area, with the harbourside cafés in view, full of tourists & locals relaxing with cool drinks. "Now that's a good idea," we thought as one.

First, we stopped for some photo opportunities with the cathedral and azure blue waters as a backdrop. Hamish pointed out a floating frisbee with 'Big Dick' emblazoned on it.

I thought about fishing it out and presenting it to him to acknowledge the invigorating walk he had just taken us on, but decided a DB was more appropriate.

It was pretty busy, but we managed to share a table with an elderly couple who left soon after we joined them. Something we said or just our perspiration smell?

The favoured Velebitsko DBs were chilled to perfection and most welcome I can tell you. The café didn't do snacks but luckily a nearby shop obliged with a jumbo pack of paprika crisps to augment our splendid beers, which went straight into the top ten most timely and refreshing beers ever.

Suitably sated, we re-traced our steps back to our hotel, looking in on the tat seller to see whether her expression indicated her mood had improved. She still looked irritated.

A quick lie down turned into two hours, the combination of early arrival, tiring walk and DB had taken their toll - we were zonked.

I awoke to Afterlife still churning out their chilled vibes on my iPod. It was now eight o'clock and we had to prise ourselves away from our pits. A quick shower to awaken the senses and we plodded out into the warm evening air.

Pasta the Sell-by Date

Our friendly host had recommended a nearby trattoria, just five minutes away. Hamish's map reading skills turned this into twenty, eventually almost stumbling across the eatery tucked away down a tiny side street.

The place was rustic - stone floor, wooden tables, paper tablecloths, strings of garlic hanging on the wall, large black & white pictures of famous Italians (Sophia Lauren, Dino Zoff, Nancy Del Olio (famous?) etc. The biggest picture of all featured an image of a smiling owner and a nonplussed looking Dean Martin.

The food was good (fresh pasta, tasty tomato sauce, aromatic basil) and the red wine most quaffable.

I nearly made a fool of myself by complaining that there was no seafood in my spaghetti Napolitano until Hamish helpfully pointed out that spaghetti marinara was the dish that I was thinking of (and had been wrongly expecting).

The restaurant was very busy and the last available table was quickly taken by a group of very bronzed middle-aged women that all turned out to be Mexicans.

They looked like an advert for Opal Fruits (a popular type of fruity sweets now known as Starburst, but which will always be known as Opal Fruits to me and my generation).

One of them was dressed top to toe in bright yellow, another in shocking green trouser suit with matching hair ribbon, a third with a lemon motif on her blouse and dangly earrings that resembled pears. Yikes!

This did not stop the equally tanned fifty-something mustachioed Italian waiter turning on the charm. He sidled across like a crab that had spotted its lunch no sooner than they had entered, and ushered the gaggle to their table with a dramatic swish of his arm.

The swarthy Latino, who had been less than responsive to us, was now all sweetness and light, an attentive servant personified.

He was soon pouring rosé wine with aplomb from a totally impractical height. He didn't spill a drop.

As you might expect of such a Latin charmer, he spoke passable Spanish. The quartet could not make up their minds what to eat so Valentino suggested the "specialità della casa", a large white fish cooked in lemon and garlic with almonds (Hamish's conversational Spanish came in unexpectedly useful).

Carlos Fandango disappeared downstairs to the kitchen and returned pronto with the uncooked sea beast that he was trying to tempt the ladies with.

He then proceeded to wave the fish on its platter in front of the ladies and spent a good five minutes explaining in detail how the delicacy would be prepared - with love naturally!

We wondered which one of the señoras he hoped to bed that night - my money was on the unfruity one, whilst Hamish fancied the lime (as the temporary winner of the lothario's heart and libido that is). If only she had been Japanese though.......

We did not wait to find out. We were bushed again and took the short route back to our beds rather than the zigzagging way we had taken to get there.

Ever the photographer, Hamish saw a shot that he intended to take with the aid of his mini tripod.

It was of the gardened square adjacent to our hotel. With its nicely lit fountain and church backdrop, it was indeed a picturesque scene. Hamish always spots them and miraculously always forgets that he is tired, hungry, ill or busting for a pee when such a photo opportunity presents itself.

As he loitered to set up the shot, something moved towards him from out of the bushes on the shadowy edge of the garden.

It transpired that it was a lady of the night. "You want sex?" she brazenly enquired of my picture-perfect pal.

"No thank you," came his ever so polite reply.

"Ohhhh, why not?" she retorted, disappointment apparent in her voice.

"I prefer the fountain," he instantly replied.

She lingered for a while, knee bent, hand on hip, chewing her gum non-alluringly. I wasn't sure whether she thought her 'sexy' stance would persuade either of us to give in to temptation or that she expected Hamish to take her photo. When neither transpired, she shuffled back behind her favourite tree.

Photo secured, bed land beckoned and was soon haven for two knackered Brits.

Coasting

We had a bus to catch next morning, along the coast to Ploče to connect with the train to Sarajevo.

We had plumped for the 11.30 to allow us some time to experience Ploče and so took breakfast at nine in the square by the gigantic Diocesan Palace ruins that dominate the Old Town.

The tourist menu that we both chose consisted of dry fried egg, watery orange juice and bitter coffee, only saved by the lovely crusty bread and a portion of la vache qui rit (cheese spread).

As we awaited the fare to arrive, I heard the telltale blast of a cruise ship's horn.

Ever the cruise spotter, I was impatient to find out what had berthed, so left Hamish to himself and walked through the underground bazaar to the water's edge.

I could make out the familiar yellow funnel of a Costa Crociere vessel and another smaller one alongside. Not too exciting (I was hoping for a monster Royal Caribbean ship or a sleek Cunard liner), so I returned to my breakfast, which was already lukewarm at best.

The bus station was alongside the train terminus, so laden with our backpacks we dodged the hordes of disembarked cruise ship passengers and headed there.

"The 11.30 is fully booked, how about the 12.30?"

We secured two of the last four seats and set about waiting for nearly two hours for it to depart.

At least I could get a good look of the cruise ships - the Costa Classica and Seabourn Spirit, described as a luxury super yacht.

Costa used to be my client when I worked for NatWest and I saw them frequently in Genoa.

I used to take photos if I saw one of their cruise ships on my travels and send them to my contacts there - probably deleted straight away, but I used to hope that one day they would find their way onto the cover of their brochure.

Deluded I know!

As we were heading to a different country, we had spent most of our Croat beans, so decided to save the little we had left for the few hours we had in Ploče.

It was a long and boring wait, but eventually the bus parked up and we boarded first. We moved twice having sat in the wrong seats, but it definitely made a pleasant change from the hard station bench.

The bus journey was as lovely as such journeys can be, following the coast for most of the way. Despite the bus being described as full, there were loads of empty seats.

The puzzle was answered when we stopped in Biokovo about half way, there a school party of early teen girls boarded and filled every seat and the aisle as well.

As hard as a chap tries, it is impossible not look at teen girl groups, barely into puberty, and assess who will be a stunner in a few years once the puppy fat and braces have gone.

Some go the wrong way (Britney Spears and Lindsay Lohan for example), but usually you can tell, as can they of course. We were no exception to the law of the bloke and were pleased to note that about 75% resembled how Milla Jovovich might have looked as a teenager!

We approached Ploče with high hopes and waited to be presented with tranquil waters and distant rolling hills

Ploče to Sarajevo – Departure 17.12 Arrival 21.05, 194KM

That's Entertainment

We arrived at the bus/train station and soon realised that we were in an industrial wasteland. No 'mini Split' as we hoped, no relaxing drink overlooking the azure blue waters. Our two-hour wait would be in decrepit surroundings sat at a scruffy café in the company of a noisy group of afternoon beer drinkers/chain-smokers.

Ploče obviously did not care that this could be a visitor's last impression of Croatia, although to be fair we later learned there was a pleasant little harbour a short taxi ride away if we had had the time, inclination and cash to bother going there (not to mention there being any taxis in the vicinity).

We were down to our last few Croatian beans as you know and calculated that we had enough for a cup of tea and a comfort break. After paying for the latter, we headed off to buy our ticket.

The ticket hall was vast with just a few plastic chairs placed in the middle of it. It reminded me of my old school assembly hall, which comfortably sat eight hundred cross-legged kids.

We wondered why such a huge building was needed. Perhaps Ploče had once been the destination of choice for the summer vacation of millions of Yugoslavs?

With Split, Dubrovnik, Kotor etc. not that far away we somehow doubted it and just put it down to the quirks of Communism. **(Subsequent research confirmed that Ploče was in fact a major hub linking holidaymakers with the Adriatic Coast).**

It was my turn to buy the train tickets, but my heart sunk when I approached the ticket window and saw a large middle-aged lady with steel rimmed glasses & bleached blonde hair sat behind the screen.

The nightmare I had faced in Sevastopol the year before came flooding back (you can read about that appalling incident in my next book).

Happily, this was to prove unfounded as she was really pleasant and spoke good English.

Unfortunately, only Croatian Kuna and not Euros or cards were accepted Fortunately I remembered that there was an ATM on the vicinity and therefore left Earos (Hamish) to watch the tickets being hand-written whilst I wandered off to secure some more beans.

Shocker - the ATM was not functioning! We were now faced with a challenge. Relatively loaded in Euro terms, but flat-broke in local denominations. I headed to the only other life around, the beery café.

The café manageress flatly refused to change any Euros. Shit, we were stuck. Out on a limb, no 'money' and no way out. Or so it seemed. Past travels in the region had taught me that there was always a way, especially if you had cash of some sort.

One of the afternoon drinkers turned out to be a businessman treating his workers to some alcoholic reward and he overheard the predicament.

Being a businessman, his exchange rates were pretty unfavourable, but I secured enough beans for the train tickets and sufficient change to upgrade the planned tea to a DB later on.

Earos was relieved to see his mate return, he had very quickly run out of small-talk and the once pleasant lady was no longer in a good mood, having written our tickets and been left wondering whether she would need to fill in a form in triplicate to explain why the transaction had not been completed.

She counted out the notes three times and held the larger denominations up to the light in case I had just manufactured a few! She made me swap one of the slightly torn ten Kuna notes (about £1) and it seemed to be almost reluctantly that she handed over our tickets out of there. Nice knowing you!

Relieved to have secured an imminent exit, we skipped back to the café for a celebratory DB. Alas they had none, so tea it was. At least this could now be supplemented with some cake and chocolate. That's living all right!

A backpacking couple from Edinburgh arrived and sat on the adjacent table. They had just arrived on the bus from Dubrovnik and were off to Mostar on the same train as us.

Adrian and Becky were also on a Balkan tour and spent their last Croatian beans on lemon beer, which was 2% proof and refreshing apparently - we took their word for it as it sounded disgusting!

Sliding Seats

With forty minutes to go before departure time the train appeared, so we decided to wander across.

The train had three coaches with one purporting to be first class. Seats secured, it was time for a few pictures of the train, its surroundings and the exterior of the cavernous ticket hall, before we impressively left exactly on time.

We soon arrived in Bosnia & Herzegovina, cue loco change and passport check. The difference this time was that our carriage was also being left behind, so off we went into the 'premium' seats after all.

You could easily see how the carriage was once luxury class. It had wood panels and large armchair like seats, it had seen better days of course, but was still pretty salubrious by most Eastern European train standards.

The only irritant was that the reclining mechanisms on the seats had obviously worn out through over use and you now had to constantly stop yourself from creeping forwards.

The old lady opposite Earos was soon virtually horizontal and before long she was asleep and snoring loudly!

Whilst it was still light, we could see impressive scenery. Rolling hills, meandering river etc. We were soon high up in the hills and looking down on towns and villages. The train tracks hugged the hillside and we travelled alarmingly close to some very sheer drops.

Opposite me sat a Bosnian chap called Matija, travelling to visit his parents in Sarajevo. He travelled with Suki, his German girlfriend and they conversed in English as their mutual language of choice. The carriage was now crowded, so the couple shared one of the recliners. Very romantic I thought.

Aside from the erratically behaving seats, the journey was quite pleasant. That was until a class full of chattering youths alighted and ruined the peace.

Worse still, there were a few heavy smokers in the party who ignored the no smoking signs. They may have had the decency to open a window, but that made the carriage decidedly chilly and much of the smoke blew back in anyway.

There was much universal tutting at this situation, but we all decided to grin and bear it rather than create a scene. They were too large a group for Hamish to even think about performing his 'hero of the train' act that he had of course successfully enacted a few years before on the trip between Bar & Podgorica.

As darkness fell, you could just about make out several dams along the river with their accompanying Hydro Electric Power stations. Far preferential to nuclear I thought.

Whether we drifted off to sleep we don't know, but both of us missed the fact that we had stopped at Mostar and we therefore assumed that we were very late. I was however soon comforted when we realised that Adrian & Becky had left the train, thus confirming that Mostar was indeed behind us.

We did in fact arrive around an hour late. 194 kilometres travelled in about five hours for an average speed of a princely forty KMH. As usual we just went with the flow.

On arrival we decided to invest in a taxi as it was pitch black and the chances of us successfully navigating the walk to the hotel or working out the tram network were slim - been there, done that etc.!

We could have chanced our arm at going ticketless on the tram again, but having gotten away with it twice before in Ukraine, we figured the law of averages was against us.

Predictably, a taxi driver wanting to know where we came from and where we were going, immediately approached us.

Apparently, City Boutique Hotel (our most expensive of the trip at €80 per night) was a long way away and would cost €10 to get there.

However, the map of Earos indicated this was a rip off and we decided that we would draw some currency and go by the meter.

The only snag was that Sarajevo train station was bereft of ATMs or an exchange office.

There was no way that we were going to give Fiddler the pleasure of agreeing his exorbitant tariff and as he was built like a shot-putter, we did not want to incur his wrath by approaching another driver in his eye-line.

In the search for a cash machine, I had noticed a rank of sorts around the corner of the station, so this is where we headed. This happened to be in complete darkness, save the dim neon of the taxi signs, so we hurriedly agreed a €5 fee - an absolute bargain we thought compared to our first quote.

We however subsequently learned that the fare should have been about half that price. Taxi drivers eh, don't you just love them!?

We soon found ourselves driving along 'Sniper Alley', a long straight road surrounded by hills. Those same hills had been alive with Bosnian Serbs during the '90s conflict, armed with rocket launchers, machine guns and Kalashnikovs, picking off Bosnia Muslims at will if they ventured outside or strayed too close to a window. The pot-marked buildings had purposely not been repaired, a stark reminder of those oh so recent horror times.

We soon passed the cubic Holiday Inn, glowing yellow in the full moonlight. The place was the permanent residence of the world's media during the Bosnian war of independence waged against the Serbs.

The siege of Sarajevo is the longest siege in the history of modern warfare, actually lasting 1,425 days from April 92 to February 96, during which time all the inhabitants of the city were confined within it.

They suffered appalling conditions in addition to living in constant fear of artillery fire.

I imagined John Simpson, the superb BBC war correspondent and veteran of all conflicts in recent memory, giving his news report as bullets whizzed by.

Having read (some of) his staggering accounts of the Gulf Wars, I made a mental note to track down a book of his memories of the Yugoslav fighting.

In fact, Simpson had been based in Belgrade during the conflict, winning a journalistic award for his writing whilst remaining there during the NATO bombing of the city in 1999.

It was actually Kate Adie and Martin Bell who had been the main BBC correspondents during the Sarajevo siege. Martin Bell's harrowing account of the war is contained in his amazing book entitled 'In Harm's Way: Bosnia, A War Reporter's Story,' that I have read since. It all certainly puts being slightly ripped off by a taxi driver into perspective!

On the Prowl

Back in the present, we were soon in central Sarajevo. We stopped at some traffic lights and I pointed out the attractive trio of females taking coffee at an adjacent café. Being Friday night, we soon noticed that the young and beautiful were out in force to see and be seen.

The twilight must have made us look better than middle-aged and nondescript, as the trio definitely looked at us looking at them. A green light soon spoilt that fantasy and before long we were checking in.

It was now past nine and Earos was getting one of his urgent need for food moments. Freshly armed with Bosnian Marks (2= €1) we set off in search of fast food.

Rejecting the corn on the cob and chestnut vendors (Hamish was not 'eat anything at all costs' starving yet), we soon found a stand-up pizza joint selling a slice for 1 BM. It was delicious too. So much so that we ventured next door to the identikit rival and bought another slice. We agreed that this would be our meal for the night and went to find a bar.

Sadly, nowhere seemed to sell DB, so it would have to be fizzy lager. What Sarajevo lacked in the beer department, it certainly made up for in the stunning girls department.

We strategically positioned ourselves to get a ringside seat as legions of lovely lasses sashayed along the street in front of us.

The girly groups just walked up and down searching for attention. We surmised that they were talent spotting before club time. Predictably we did not constitute talent, as with no panes of glass or twilight to mask us, our true likeness was revealed!

I was reminded of my times sat at bars and restaurants along Miami's Ocean Drive with my colleagues from my banking cruise team.

This too was a place for 'talent spotting' and although I still wasn't A or even G list material back then in my pre-marriage late '90s, I liked to think that I was at least a junior contender. In all likelihood I was deluded to think so. At least now I knew my true place!

We noticed that the corn and nut vendor was doing a fairly brisk trade. He too was in a strategic position, enabling him to meet his twin need for sales and sighting female flesh.

He was a good twenty years older than us, but with a very acute roving eye. We even acknowledged each other with a knowing smile when a particularly tight pair of shorts walked by!

Neither of us could stomach more than two gassy glasses of lager, so despite the floorshow we somehow decided we needed some ice cream.

Frustratingly all the shops we had seen selling a delicious variety of gelato had shut for the night, so we were left with a McFlurry as the only option.

So, my first ever McDonalds ice cream was to be eaten in Bosnia. I chose the smarties variety (Hamish went for Kit Kat), which I firmly believed would be my last one (and it still is).

Pretty ghastly as it happened and I am sure this had nothing to do with the local method of production – I could just as easily have been in Copenhagen, Cairo or Croydon.

Fatal for Franz

After yet another cheese-orientated breakfast synonymous with these trips, it was time to explore. First job though was to return to the train station to secure tickets for Sunday's departure to Belgrade.

In the light of day, we were able to take the tram with tickets purchased from a nearby kiosk.

In 1885 Sarajevo had the honour of being the first city in Europe (and second in the world after San Francisco) to get full-time electric trams, just after the city became part of the Austro-Hungary Empire.

The Empire had wanted trams in Vienna, however they decided upon somewhere else to be the guinea pig in case it all went horribly wrong. The tram that we found ourselves on seemed to date from that time, a fabulous rickety affair that was full of character & history.

Train ticket secured with no drama whatsoever, we trammed it back as far as the Latin Bridge before alighting. This is one of the world's most famous bridges. Not for rivaling Prague's Karlovy Most or the Golden Gate of San Francisco for architectural

168

majesty, but as the spot where Arch Duke Franz Ferdinand and his wife Sofia were gunned down by Bosnian-Serb Gavrilo Principe in June 1914.

Ferdinand was heir to the Austro-Hungarian throne and his assassination led to the events that started World War One, as countries honoured their various treaties and pacts.

After a few pics at this historic place, we then went for a pleasant stroll alongside the River Miljacka, passing the impressive city hall and spotting where the city brewery was located (handy for later), finally arriving at Baščaršija, (the Old Town), once known as the Jerusalem of Europe due to the fact the Jewish, Islamic & Christian faiths have all been worshipped there for centuries.

In a very similar layout to Mostar, the old town area was now home to shops selling colourful goods such as lamps and textiles, artisan workshops, cafés, guesthouses and market stalls.

It was also the site of two important mosques and a very impressive Moorish-style fountain made of intricately carved wood atop a stone plinth and steps.

This was a great place to stroll. Worship and trade had been carried out here since the Ottomans set up the area in the 15th century. It seemed that little had changed in that respect, except perhaps for the betting shop positioned opposite the main mosque entrance.

One old guy dressed in a dirty overcoat, ancient leather cap and worn out steel toe-capped boots sat outside working out his betting selections. By the look of his attire and odorous smell, he needed some luck!

There was even a fantastic shop selling nothing but the fez, the wonderfully evocative red headgear, complete with black tassel, named after the Moroccan city that is credited with its invention.

"Just like that", I thought out loud, remembering the hilarious and bizarre late British comedian Tommy Cooper, who always wore a fez on stage & screen.

He was one of those comedians that only had to walk on stage and grin inanely to get audiences in stitches. His trademark was to do magic tricks that always went wrong (despite him really being an accomplished magician).

His catch phrase was "just like that". Hamish had no idea why his pal was smiling broadly as the image of the lanky buffoon crossed my mind.

Ever a sucker for colourful things and with a view to appeasement for my homecoming, I bought some exquisite cushion covers, before we settled down for a Turkish coffee in a traditional little tearoom opposite the side entrance to the main mosque.

As we sat, a large Christian group led by two clergymen paraded past singing hallelujah and making music on drums and guitars. The European Jerusalem notion lives on, I thought.

This was time to chill out and just watch the world go by outside the tiny teashop that was barely big enough for three small tables.

Men played backgammon on a small table opposite, Muslims came to pray in the mosque, women carried heavy bags laden with goods, either just bought or destined to be sold, a tour group followed a leader holding a radio aerial with a blue ribbon tied around it.

Why do they have to do that? We get the follow the leader bit and the need for that leader to hold something up to be seen in the crowds.

The bit we can never fathom out however, is why people want to be herded around and be told what to do and when to do it, as well as having all of those instantly forgotten facts and figures shoved down their throats. Who actually enjoys that?

Jewell in the Crown

As we contemplated that conundrum (an edition of LP and independence being the preference every time for this thrifty duo), we had a second strong and bitter coffee. As it was Saturday, it was Premier League football back in England and my Manchester City were away to Fulham, just as had been the case on our previous years' trip.

My mobile WIFI confirmed that City were losing one-nil to a debatable penalty. Remarkably I stayed chilled.

"Fancy a DB in the brewery", I enquired of Hamish. No hard sell was required as Hamish readily accepted the suggestion as a way to wash away the pervasive 'coffee mouth' that now engulfed our taste buds.

Sarajevska Pivara to give it the correct name was opened in 1864 and by the look of it was totally unscathed in all of the hostilities. We speculated that the Bosnian Serbs wanted to keep the place in tact in case they thwarted the Islamist independence bid and had wanted somewhere to celebrate their victory.

Covering a large area close to the river, right opposite St Anthony's Church (very handily placed for dissipating the taste of communion wine!), the colourful building was impossible to miss. Its burnt red and yellow exterior reminding us of those fruit salad penny chews from the UK that were on sale in the 19'70s.

The interior was equally impressive. A large dimly lit theatre of beer with wooden-paneled walls, shiny wooden floors, a ten-metre long curved bar, huge beer barrels scattered randomly to act as tables, and an upstairs balcony that ensured that the entire space was suitably maximised.

The service was also pretty wooden as it took an age to be acknowledged by a waiter. Whilst we waited, we read our LP guidebook.

"The Brewery played an important role in Sarajevo life during the war. When the Serb forces cut electricity, gas, and water supplies to the city, people were fearful about taking the water from the river and would come to fill drums and buckets from the deep spring on the brewery grounds, which was the only source of fresh water in the besieged city."

We further learned that the brewery buildings were in fact damaged during the siege but had been lovingly restored to their former glory. As our first DB arrived, Manchester City equalised; things were definitely looking up. The beer was excellent and City had scored, magic.

We decided to celebrate with a snack. Such were the portion sizes of our hors d'oeuvres consisting of chips, cheese croquettes & mushroom sauce, that the snack turned into our main calorific meal, royally augmented with delicious crusty bread and the DB.

As we were tucking in, Edin Džeko, Manchester City's Bosnian striker, scored a late winner at Craven Cottage. Time for another DB!

How apt that City's Bosnian striker who had been born in Sarajevo and who started his career at local club FK Željezničar (then the current Bosnian champions), should score such an important goal whilst I was visiting his birthplace.

As we waddled back through the Old Town, I was stopped by several locals to acknowledge the fact that I was wearing a City shirt, for whom the local hero (known in these parts as the Bosnian Diamond) had just scored.

I turned down all offers for the shirt and instead took a couple of photos, one of a poster advertising the national team's forthcoming international match in Greece featuring an image of said striker, and another of a rail of dodgy replicas of Džeko's Bosnian shirt that were up for sale.

Amazingly Džeko shirts outsold global megastars Lionel Messi & Cristiano Ronaldo by three to one.

We returned to the hotel for a wash & brush up before we entered the catwalk once more. We managed to watch Fashion TV (a staple of our trips whenever available) for twenty minutes to get some practice on how to impress, but sadly we were very poor pupils and our clothes were badly in need of an iron.

No DB to be found anywhere once more, so it was déjà vu as we again sat on those same stools with a great window on the world. It may have been late September, but shirtsleeves were the order of the day and pleasingly many of the ladies wore even less.

Despite the gassy beer and irritating euro-trance-pop, we were to stay here for a good couple of hours. The corn vendor gave us a nod like we were familiar friends returning to our local. His trade was even brisker that night.

It was very noticeable that the young people out and about that night were just out for a nice time. Frugally just drinking a coffee, consuming an ice cream or partaking of the odd beer, no doubt to be followed by some energetic moves on various dance floors.

None of the binge drinking that blights UK towns and cities every weekend. We lamented as to why we have adopted that culture, with women often worse culprits than men.

We touched on the likes of teenage pregnancies and our blighted reputation abroad before we realised that we were sounding like Muppet moaners Waldorf and Statler, so promptly returned to sightseeing!

A couple of fairly attractive ladies in their early forties sat in front of us. A great pity that they smoked or their luck could have been in with newly single Hamish!

To their left sat four women that were of similar age, but definitely not in the oil painting category. They also smoked, but Hamish would not have been interested anyway!

They did attract a man in his sixties though. With his shabby black suit, scuffed shoes and dandruff shoulders, he scuttled over from the other side of the road, box of custard cream biscuits in one hand and ancient tape recorder in the other.

He offered the less than fab four a biscuit, an offer that all four accepted. It seemed as though the biscuits accompanied their cocktails wonderfully as they then engaged in conversation for the next hour.

"I will give you a pound if you go and buy some jaffa cakes and offer them to the women and another pound if they invite you to join them for a cocktail," I dared Hamish. We had another beer instead!

Then came the crucial point. The man gestured to his tape recorder and appeared to be inviting one or more of the ladies to a wicked house party at his gaff.

Unfortunately for him he seemed to fail with his invitation as he soon scuttled off again, no doubt to buy some chocolate bourbons or some such like and find another prospect elsewhere.

Ten out of ten for effort though!

We decided that signalled the end of the night's entertainment for us as well.

There was just time to take a couple of good night photographic shots before returning the few metres back to our boutique hotel.

There was another early start to come next day as were headed to Serbia and its capital Belgrade.

Chapter Seven – So Near, Sofia

We had kept just enough beans for the tram to the station and some basic supplies for the train journey to Belgrade.

There was an hour or so to kill before we needed to depart, so we decided to take a last look at the Old Town, just waking up after the previous night's excesses.

As we strolled, we noticed that some workers were doing some maintenance to a small stretch of tramline. The hotel confirmed our fears that there would be no trams that day due to planned engineering work. A reminder of home that we could have done without.

Damn, did this mean that we needed more beans?

As it happened, a taxi was no more expensive than two tram tickets, at least until the inevitable extras were added on plus rounding!

We had just enough, but our surplus for supplies was severely diminished. Just as well we had purloined some DIY cheese rolls from the breakfast table.

Sarajevo to Belgrade Departure 11.35 Arrival 20.18, 330KM

From one capital to another in former Yugoslavia, this time the big one, the actual capital of the Slavic nation that stuck together against all odds under the leadership of General Tito.

Bygones

The particular train line had not been operational for eighteen years, only reopening in late 2009. The 'Olympic Express' was now a symbol of moving forward and putting the past firmly in the past.

The daytime journey had given us the opportunity to savour the passing countryside and have a few decent conversations with locals along the way.

It was also the journey that I really started to notice the wheeltappers.

At every stop three or four men or women armed with a long wooden handled hammer tapped every wheel, listening out for the tell-tale sign of a crack in one of the wheels.

It took years of practice apparently to detect the slight difference in resonance that indicated a cracked wheel, so my train-spotting pal helpfully explained.

A crack can happen at any time, a bit like on your car windscreen. A slight crack means that the train can carry on and be repaired later. A serious crack however could lead to a time-consuming repair or carriage detachment that would put you seriously behind schedule.

Happily, we got the all clear at every station. The tappers were to become a prominent feature on every journey from now on. I was amazed that I hadn't consciously noticed them before on previous trips.

We had the same system in the UK up until a few decades ago, but this particular art form has been confined to Western European history now that expensive diagnostic computer systems in the driver's cab let it be known if there is even the slightest issue (thanks to Hamish for the info once more)! Not quite an airline flight deck, but not far off.

Take One

Jazek, a film student on his way back to university, joined us in our compartment. As a Serb he was interested on what we thought of his country.

We sensed he wanted to discuss our thoughts on the war, no doubt in the knowledge that Serbia was portrayed as bullying aggressors in much of the media during that time.

We however tactically swerved that particular subject and gave the usual 'lovely country, friendly people', quotes. I decided against recounting our Niš experience!

Our conversation soon turned to film, photography, travel and a mutual admiration for Milla Jovovich.

Jazek was a militant student. He travelled without a ticket. "Let them fucking try and arrest me, fucking regime." He evidently knew how to dodge the ticket inspector, as he claimed to have never bought a public transport ticket and never been fined either.

He advised us to ride the trams for free as nobody ever checked. I sensed it would be fruitless to argue that an obvious foreigner boarding at the main train station would be fair game for a fine, so just thanked him for the advice.

As we approached central Belgrade, we passed an impressive suspension bridge, known as the Blue Bridge (real name Plavi Most) crossing the Sava River. "The most fucking expensive bridge in the whole of Europe," lambasted Jazek. "Fucking regime."

He volunteered to show us where to get the 'free' tram that would take us to near our hotel. He patiently waited while we changed some money before leading us to the tram. Despite his friendliness, I hoped he would leave us to it now. I wanted to buy a ticket and I somehow felt this would deeply offend him.

"Why you ignore my advice, why you waste your money," I could imagine him accusing.

Our tram was due in eight minutes. After three, Jazek announced his own tram had arrived and hopped on, after handshakes all round. This gave us about four minutes to get tickets. With no sign of anywhere to get them, we asked a friendly looking guy where we could make the purchase.

"Don't worry about it, there won't be inspectors at this time of night," came the familiar sounding reply.

So, we nervously travelled four ticketless stops before bailing out with the Holiday Inn in sight. Once more we were on tenterhooks for no need. One day I am sure we will not be quite so lucky.

Hamish's hotel loyalty points had scored again, albeit that we seemed in the middle of nowhere. He had virtually lived his life for two years in a Holiday Inn in the UK due to working away from home. This had made him an Elite Member and possessor of several hundred thousand reward points.

When the receptionist handed us a piece of paper on behalf of the management to apologise for the fact that the restaurant was out of use due to a private function, we did start to wonder quite where we would eat that night.

Luckily there was a pizza place about ten-minutes' walk away and this was where we headed once we had made a sizeable dent in the free minibar (it was great staying with the elite!).

Not only did the restaurant have wonderful pizzas, but they also served Albanian Korça, one of our all-time favourite DBs. What a find!

Two of those beauties each went down really well - we were a little disappointed that we had drunk their last four bottles, which sadly meant no take-outs for the next night's train journey.

Serb Saunter

Next day we set off around eight headed for the train station. As we walked towards the tram stop, we came across what appeared to be the facade of a building, which we presumed at first to be a preserved structure of great importance.

Closer inspection showed that the facade was in fact made of wood - we had stumbled across a deserted film set.

It looked to be set up for something set in a yesteryear era. We speculated that the gorgeous Milla might appear at any moment -

wishful thinking of course.

Hamish recounted the time that he had stumbled across filming in Bristol for a period drama.

He had been intrigued by some really bright lights when out for a midnight stroll, so made a beeline for them. Incredibly they were shooting a floodlit daytime scene in the empty city.

Typically, Hamish had no idea what drama was being shot or who the actors were. If it had been a cartoon version of Downton Abbey, he would have been right on the money!

We headed for the train station to book our tickets for later and to leave our bags so to be luggage free for our exploration. Again, we went ticketless on the tram as there was simply no place to buy them. Even the hotel concierge advised we didn't need one.

Did public transport make any money in Serbia!?

We resembled meerkats as we looked around for possible ticket inspectors. Our hearts sank as a guy got on wearing an official looking badge, however if he was an inspector, he was a pretty poor one!

We purchased our tickets for the train to Sofia easily enough. We were informed however that we could not secure our sleeping berth and would need to see the guard thirty minutes before departure to reserve this element of our journey.

We found this bizarre - what if a coach load of Japanese tourists turned up and reserved all the beds? We however put all thoughts of a sleepless journey aside and headed for left luggage.

This was a typical affair - two burly ruffians, a dirty concrete room with metal shelves, an open window to pass your bags through and sign written in black marker pen showing the prices per twenty-four hours, together with the proclamation 'Do Not Loose (sic) Your Ticket.'

Two English female student travellers were before us but were disappointed to learn that credit cards were not accepted. They will learn!

Very helpful of the baggage handlers not to mention that payment was due when the luggage was collected - if only they had an ounce of customer service in their make up!

We had spurned the €15 hotel breakfast so went for the €4 railway café version. A delicious enormous cheese salad baguette and a strong coffee. Bargain.

It was a short walk to the centre despite a taxi driver trying to convince us otherwise. He was well up on his football - I sported my Manchester City shirt again and he reeled off the names of current City players Kolarov & Nastasić (both Serbian) Džeko and Italian manager Roberto Mancini. Despite his knowledge, we still preferred to walk.

We headed for the citadel area high above the city with splendid views along the rivers Danube and Sava, including the point where they flowed into one another.

We were to be blessed with unseasonably good weather for the whole trip and this day was the hottest of the lot at 32C. This meant beautiful clear skies so that you could see for miles around.

We had a dicey tram moment on the way up with me having to squash myself into a hedge to avoid being struck. We soon realised that we were walking in an area designed for trams only.

Both of us were completely deafened but thankful all the same for the tram driver sounding his horn, no doubt to let us know that we were out of bounds.

The sprawling fortress was a haven from the busy city below. Hamish and I boosted the visitor numbers into double figures, peace and quiet for all.

Hamish suddenly stopped in his tracks. The reason? A beautiful girl of South-East Asian extraction, being photographed by a white haired and bearded man at least forty years her senior.

All body language indicated they were an item. An obvious case of Thai bride. The virtues of mail order wife were there for all to see - he would get ten years company from a stunning girl whilst she would inherit a huge camera when he popped his clogs.

For an obvious reason, our tour of the citadel followed the same route as the odd couple, only twenty metres distance apart. Hamish stayed very quiet from then on!

Eventually the novelty sort of wore off and we decided an ice cream was in order. When she followed suit and suggestively licked her cornet, Hamish once again fell silent.

On the way down back towards the centre, we passed the military museum. We didn't go in but did explore the outside collection of captured NATO tanks and artillery. I was surprised that they hadn't demanded them back.

We strode past the tacky souvenir stalls and I got my second ever sighting of a black squirrel, before we soon found ourselves in the bustling pedestrian area of shops and cafés.

The commercial centre of Belgrade was a hive of activity - shoppers, café dwellers, buskers, beggars, flower-sellers.

We stopped at an Italian style café for a coffee. The place was full of pretty people - our faces may not have fitted, but this didn't stop us enjoying a refreshing forty-five minutes.

Having perused the shops, we returned to the same pit stop for our main meal of the day and more observation.

I used the disinfectant gel that Mrs Wilbur insisted I bring with me. On shaking the bottle, I was annoyed that the lid came off and horrified to see some gel had flown out and now sat on the back of an expensive looking jacket of a well to do female diner.

I held my breath ready for the reaction. This never came however. Phew, she hadn't noticed and neither had her heavily made-up companion.

I figured silence was the best policy even if it may have left a stain. If that makes me a bad person I apologise, but being a coward seemed preferable to being a martyr and causing a fuss in this situation.

The pasta was great as was the DB. With two hours to go until train time, we decided to wander down to the station. We were both concerned about the sleeping situation and wished to secure our beds as soon as possible.

This didn't stop us going into every convenience store and latterly every café to try and secure DB for the journey. This drew a blank, but we were confident one of the station kiosks would come up trumps.

We found the guard with ninety minutes to go until show time. He told us to return in an hour and indicated that he would hold two berths for us. We just hoped that a fistful of yen wouldn't persuade him otherwise.

Plenty of time to avail ourselves of DB. No luck at the train station and we were to remain frustrated despite trying a dozen or more places at the adjacent bus station.

Eventually we found a mini market that had a litre of DB in a dusty plastic bottle – obviously not a popular purchase in those parts. The beer was enthusiastically purchased along with accompanying junk food. We were now set. Except we were now also lost!

We walked in circles but could not retrace our steps back to the train station. We had to take a taxi for the five-minute ride. This cost us €5 as we had no beans left apart from our rucksack retrieval costs and the driver would not accept crackers as payment!

The guard showed us to our berth and wrote us out a sleeping supplement for €14 between us. No change of course, so €15 it was then.

The bed may have been rock hard, but it beat an upright night on a seat in a crowded carriage any day.

Belgrade to Sofia Departure 21.50 Arrival 08.04, 401KM

This time the journey to Sofia was far more pleasurable than it had been a few years before. On this occasion we were only to be three hours late as well as happily being in relatively warm comfort throughout.

Earache

We hoped we would be lucky enough to get the four-berth compartment to ourselves. We nervously watched several large travellers board the train, but luckily the guard was practicing his own form of segregation, which came up trumps for us. Perhaps the €1 'tip' had come in very worthwhile for us.

So only familiar snores and snorts for us that night, quite a relief.

Next door, two French guys 'bagged' a rather pretty Canadian girl. Cue ridiculous attempts by the young lads to try and woo the lass. I suffered for what seemed an age as their benign questioning and abysmal attempt at rapport filtered into our direction.

Such gems as "do you know France", "have you been to Bulgaria before", "do you like Canada" and "can I share your berth" (OK, I lied for the last one but that is what they were thinking and at least it would have made the conversation a tiny bit interesting!).

As we left Belgrade, we followed the river past the expensive blue lit bridge and out towards our hotel, before switching back and over said bridge to head off to Bulgaria.

This involved our loco breaking rank and heading off to the near distance, only to return straight past us and off into the near distance the other way, before finally reversing back and hitching up to the carriages again. We had gone from the back of the train to being right at the front - this was to be a bad move for us later.

The inane conversation next door eventually died down. I had decided to block most of their chatter with Blancmange in my ears - the sitar inspired '80s pop group rather than the sickly dessert.

We celebrated the silence by draining our DB (Hamish had decanted half into an empty water bottle), before attempting sleep.

We passed Niš in the dead of night, but this was where the train split with the other half off to Skopje. Such was the jolting of the detachments and the vigour of the shunting back and forth that I was rudely awakened. The curse of Niš strikes again!

To add to the discomfort, they decided to change the loco again and being right behind it now, we bore the full brunt of the bumps in the night.

Hamish gave a few snorts but clearly remained asleep. Lucky git. I looked at my watch. We were already ninety minutes late. Here we go again..........

Further along, another very violent loco change together with some stern border guards at the Bulgarian border stirred us once more. The train then seemed to wait an age before moving off again. It was now just about daylight so feeling defeated, I looked out of the window to see what was going on.

The sight of the train guard carrying an armful of burgers and a cardboard tray of coffee met me. He could have fed half the train with that lot! As soon as he re-boarded, we were off again.

I imagined the announcement we would have got in England.

"Slavic Railways apologise for the delay to your journey which has been caused by excessive shunting in Niš, a peckish train crew at Dimitrovgrad and a faulty deep fat fryer. This train is now 170 minutes late, we apologise once again for the inconvenience this may cause you!"

At least the chirpy Gallic pals did not strike up again, so sleep soon returned - it was only 6.30 after all.

The last leg was a crawl as commuters from Sofia's suburbs joined us. Once more our scruffy clothes mixed with smart suits and dresses, albeit we were sealed off out of sight in our messy sleeper. At last we arrived.

Anti-Climax

We had pre-booked accommodation, so headed straight for it by taxi. Although the hotel was a shabby affair, it turned out to have fantastic breakfasts with a comprehensive array of bread, cheeses and hams. Excellent ingredients for some wonderful home-made sandwiches for our next journey.

We found Sofia drab and uninteresting. The vast modern Nevsky Cathedral that had been completed in the early 20th century, looked interesting from a distance with its huge golden dome and lesser green versions, but on closer inspection and a look inside it had flattered to deceive somewhat.

We soon became bored and glad we were off the next day for two nights in Veliko Tarnovo.

That night, we headed past the nicely lit Sheraton and the Tzum department store for the pedestrian Vitosha Street.

This was the street of restaurants, bars and nightclubs. No sooner had we left the underpass to emerge at the start of the entertainment street than a grotty looking gypsy girl, who looked about thirteen, approached us.

She first asked for a cigarette and then almost immediately offered us sex. No givers or takers for either thank you.

The first 'night club' we passed was called Cupid. A femme fatale dressed all in black, save for her red stilettos, beckoned us inside what was evidently a lap-dancing club. No thanks.

"Perhaps later?" she countered. Perhaps not we both thought. We only wanted a pizza and a beer, it was Tuesday for goodness sake!

After food, we sat at an outside bar for a refreshing DB named Stolichno. The street was long and not purpose built to be pedestrianised. Tram tracks bisected the road, which was seemingly all geared up for transport. It could clearly be de-pedestrianised very quickly.

For now, we sat traffic free and slowly sipped away. Once more the young and lovely surrounded us. Oh, how we must have stood out.

With an early start next morning, it was off to bed before eleven -

we would return Friday night when we supposed the place would be much livelier and so we hoped would we be.

Spurning the advances of the grubby teenager for second time, we soon arrived back at our hotel.

Next morning, after leaving our main rucksacks and armed with our DIY fodder purloined from the breakfast table, we decided to walk to the train station. It took a brisk thirty-minutes, but was excellent for clearing away any stiffness that remained in our bodies.

We would also be sat for the next four hours, so the exercise was most welcome.

Sofia to Gorna Oryakhovitsa Departure 10.05 Arrival 14.17, 294KM

We arrived at Gorna, the gateway to Veliko Tarnovo, right on time - a first for Bulgarian Rail in our experience. I had slept much of the 4-hour journey, figuring that I would see the countryside on the return leg.

Unfortunately, the picturesque branch line was closed for repairs, so there were three buses waiting to transport people to various destinations. We were directed to one of them and prayed we had been understood and were on the correct one.

Our anxiety increased when the other two left almost immediately to leave us on our lonesome. Thirty minutes later we had not moved - the driver was on his lunch break!

Run VT

We eventually set off for the half hour journey. We were a little alarmed when the driver seemed to ignore the Veliko Tarnovo sign and head in the opposite direction to that indicated. Panic over when a few minutes later there was another VT sign, which this time the driver obeyed.

As this was a rail replacement bus, it took us to the train station, a mile and a half up hill to the centre. This was despite the fact that every passenger wanted the centre and it would have been just as easy to drop us there.

Before we had time to gather our bearings and thoughts, every car and taxi had zoomed off leaving us behind alone.

The train info desk was open despite there being no trains at present, coming or going. The pleasant lady confirmed that buses to and from the station had also been temporarily suspended. As she could not stir us a taxi, we would be walking!

Hamish confidently advised the direction in which we should go. I was sceptical, but pleasingly he was correct.

So, a forty-minute yomp uphill in the early afternoon heat ensued - good practice as it turned out for the next day's activities.

We crossed the bridge over the River Yantra and soon found ourselves in the centre.

Our hotel also boasted a spa and we both availed ourselves of an invigorating massage later on that afternoon. No funny business you understand!

We dumped our bags as usual - hotel wardrobes rarely get used on our trips together.

Veliko was fairly compact - the main reason people came there was as a base for the fortress of Tsaravets on the outskirts of town, and the monasteries high up in the hills.

That was all to be for the next day's exertions - today was about chilling and hopefully taking in the Manchester City v Borussia Dortmund Champions League match on TV that night.

Salad and a very pleasant DB (this one branded Ariana) was just the ticket for now. We were peckish rather than hungry. I had made myself two Scooby snack style rolls at breakfast, both eaten en route from Sofia - two types of ham, some laughing cow, smoked cheese, gherkin, cucumber and tomato. Superb. Hamish had the same excluding the ham of course, being vegetarian.

Now it was time to return to the hotel for R&R. Not before Hamish had taken a photo of a goofy looking pink dinosaur in the local toy shop. Little things.......

Hamish took the plunge at the spa first. A fair-haired girl in her twenties dressed in a white tunic took the order for an oil massage for about €30 - she would also be the masseuse.

They did have a chocolate version available, but Hamish figured he would attract wasps later on if he had partaken in that one, so went for the more traditional variety. I wished him luck before returning to my room to contemplate whether to have one myself.

A nice hot shower left me in relaxed mood, and I had nodded off by the time Hamish returned. He described the massage as sensational.

I decided that I would also go for it. €30 very well spent indeed as the ruck sack stiffness was erased from my back and shoulders. I floated back to the room and like Hamish I was soon slumbering noisily.

That evening was footie night. We first went for a beer in a music bar that attracted us by playing Stone Roses & Oasis. The bar TV also showed the City match.

We were tempted to stay but as the match started at 9.45 and it would be close to midnight by the time it had finished, we thought we had better find a restaurant that also had it on.

Bingo! Next door to that afternoon's pizza joint came up trumps. We took in the match noshing on pasta and swigging by now familiar Stolichno DB.

The evening was notable for two things - firstly, City were totally outplayed and only drew 1-1 due to an unbelievable display by their goalkeeper Joe Hart and a well dodgy penalty near the end, and secondly everybody apart from the two of us were chain smoking.

So much so, that despite the fact that we sat outside our eyes were streaming, our noses blocked, and our clothing smelt like ashtrays.

Time for bed said Zebedee and there were no arguments from us, as we could hardly keep our smoke injured eyes open.

Going Up

We woke to yet another beautiful sunny day. We were soon raring to go and headed off towards Tsaravets.

We ambled through the main town and out along a cobbled street lined with craft shops and cafés. There were many colourful souvenirs to be had at low prices - shopping later!

As we started to walk down the hill, a gap in the buildings gave us our first view of the fortress, and impressive it looked too in the morning sunshine.

Armed with a basic tourist map, we decided we would walk seven kilometres to the hilltop monastery first and return to the main tourist site later.

So, past the stronghold walls we went and down into the valley below. The scene was very picturesque with an ancient church and stone bridge with the glistening Yantra River flowing beneath it. We could see the branch line from Gorna - it would have made for a lovely journey.

We hit the main road up the winding hill at around eleven. A busy road it was too, meaning we had to continually look out for vehicles that due to the road layout were usually coming on our side from behind us.

The road was long, and the sun was hot. It took eighty minutes to get to the top by which time our remaining water was very warm, and we were pretty tired and sweaty. Once again raisins helped to keep us going. Thanks again for looking after me Mrs Wilbur.

A sign beckoned us along a rough road off the main track towards St Nikolai Monastery. This was a further thirty-minute walk, but well worth the effort.

With its lovely garden, white washed buildings and antique church, it made for a lovely tranquil setting. The heavily scented and brightly coloured plants attracted a multitude of bees, which I stood and watched for a good ten minutes or so. Hamish was really pleased that he had no traces of chocolate on him.

Nuns and monks went about their business of sweeping, gardening, cooking and cleaning, seemingly totally oblivious to our presence. I did have some interaction with a nun in the church when I purchased a small icon of St Nicholas, but the few words spoken during the transaction were the only ones uttered during our forty-minute visit.

We had been the only non-residents there and only as we left did another small group arrive.

Above the monastery stood a new looking hotel, where we decided to head in search of refreshment.

The hotel restaurant had a veranda and it was here we sat. The view was fantastic. Down past the terracotta roofs of the monastery to the valley below, with Tsaravets looking majestic set against a green backdrop. The eye was then drawn up again to the roofs and spires of VT.

A meal of Greek salad, fried cheese and garlic pitta bread washed down with coke hit the spot marvellously and we lingered for over an hour to recharge the batteries and take in the spectacular view.

There was one blot on the landscape. Above the monastery on the other side stood a really ugly hotel. We were amazed that the local planners had approved such a carbuncle that was totally out of keeping with the sartorial elegance of every other structure.

We started talking to some middle-aged Spanish holiday-makers who came there every year and I mentioned the hideous hotel. One of the ladies explained that this used to be the summer retreat of the Communist Party leaders. No planning permission necessary there then obviously!

From the hotel we wandered into the village of Arbanassi to replenish our water supplies and stroll around the pretty paths and basic roads. The main road that we had walked up cut through the village and today was white line painting day.

An army of eight painters seemed to consist of seven supervisors and one workman, and even he wasn't exactly breaking sweat. It would be a long job.

We decided against going to the village museum and agreed we would take a taxi down as far as the Tsaravets entrance.

When we got there Hamish pointed out that the light was no longer optimum, so the decision was taken that we would return next day before our afternoon train back to Sofia.

We soon found ourselves in craft shop alley. I bought three ornate mustard/jam pots with wooden spoons (couldn't work out why when I got them home), a ceramic coaster and a cobalt blue pottery necklace for Mrs Wilbur. I stayed to talk to the artist and watched her intricately hand decorating her clay creations with a scalpel. She was very good at her vocation.

Hamish bought two hand carved wooden storks with orange beaks. They were a whopping €25 each, but he bartered down to €40 for the pair, which he promptly christened Veliko and Tarnovo.

After a coffee and calorific cake sat overlooking the river, we took ourselves and our purchases back to the hotel to recuperate for our last night in VT and penultimate night of the trip.

Farewell My Friend

First to the music bar, this time for Verve, Mansun and Blur, then onto the Italian and we finally ended up in a blues/rock bar named Melon.

There was to be no live music that night, with the resident drum kit remaining silent, but the place rocked to Hendrix, U2 and the Doors. Hamish resisted my offer to pay him a pound for an impromptu drum solo!

The bar was decorated with black and white pictures of Jimi, the Beatles, Morrison, the Who, Jagger, Joplin, Clapton, Queen and Floyd. All Americans or British (I count Freddie Mercury as honorary English despite him hailing from Zanzibar). Our conversation that night was around how these countries dominated popular music since rock n' roll had begun in the early fifties.

With Canada, Jamaica and Australia forming the 'B' Division, it was clear that the English language was a primary factor, but this could not totally explain why all the greats seemed to be from USA or UK.

I suppose it made up for the fact that Elgar and Copland are considered second-rate, when compared to Mozart, Beethoven and Tchaikovsky in the classical music stakes.

To explore this fully would take a book on its own and perhaps I am being biased against Europeans through ignorance, but there was not a photo of the Scorpions or Roxette to be seen!

So, our last night in VT was spent drinking beer, making good conversation and listening to brilliant music. What more is there to life?

Final Fling

Our last full day of the trip arrived with the sun shining once more. Our train back to Sofia was at three, giving us time to visit Tsaravets before catching the bus to Gorna.

This was a proper fortress. A gradually inclining path led us to the gatehouse with its fine portcullis. We walked around the thick-walled fort with a childlike spring in our step, as usual declining the audio guide and preferring to leave things to our own imaginations.

The Bulgarian flag fluttered proudly in the breeze adjacent to the church, which was the centre point of the complex.

Unfortunately, it was locked as we found out at about the same time as a large school party of six-year-olds who had clambered up the steps with their teachers.

While they chattered noisily, we headed down to the little café for a coffee. From here you could see the rock protruding from part of the wall where jailers forced prisoners and wrong doers to jump to their deaths.

Sadly, it was soon time to depart. Neither of us really wanted to go back to Sofia and wished we could have flown home from here. Alas our flight was from the capital, plus we had left our main rucksacks in our hotel so we could travel light to VT.

The scene as we left the fortress compound made us smile.

There was a replica horse and a box of fancy-dress clothes. The kids that we had seen earlier took it in turns to dress up as knights and princesses for a souvenir photo of their visit.

They looked so cute in their headdresses and helmets, mounted on their steed as they made what they believed to be regal or knightly expressions whilst posing for the camera.

Shortly after that we found ourselves on the scheduled bus to Gorna. I loved the fact that our fare came to four-lev, which meant we were given a blue ticket and a red ticket each, one representing three lev and the other one lev.

After selling all the passengers their different coloured tickets depicting the value of their journeys, the conductor sat down, retrieved a large book from the side of her seat and meticulously wrote down every transaction.

This was some feat. Not only did she remember all the various journeys with the appropriate fares, but she also managed to write everything incredibly neatly, anticipating every bump along the route. I felt like giving her a round of applause such was her artistry in trying circumstances.

We arrived with seventy minutes to spare, not wanting to cut it too fine. Having obtained our standard class tickets, we decided to take lunch.

Choice was limited as you can imagine, but a small café just outside the station provided sustenance with cheese omelette and chips.

I sniffed the oil the food had been cooked in\with before eating, having been a food poisoning victim in Bolivia when eating the exact same meal. The test was passed and very nice the food was too.

Gorna Oryakhovitsa to Sofia Departure 14.28 Arrival 18.51, 294KM

We strolled to the platform to find it pretty crowded. It was Friday afternoon and clearly Sofia was a popular destination for the weekend.

Furthermore, when the train arrived it was packed already. We scrambled aboard with the best of them and managed to find two seats in a compartment.

As we set off, we realised we were in first class. Hamish set off to explore whether there were spares in standard. He returned fifteen minutes later to report standing room only and not much of this left either. We decided to stay put and take our chances.

A further ten minutes passed before the female ticket inspector arrived. She checked her book - we were in luck; our seats were unreserved and for a four-lev supplement each we could nab them.

The inspector was a very sexy lady and she knew it.

In her early forties, she was tall with long legs extenuated by short skirt. She also knowingly possessed an ample bosom, leaving her shirt unbuttoned sufficiently to reveal a good deal of cleavage. She tossed back her thick black mane, before sitting on the vacant seat in front of me.

She was well made up and could best be described as a taller and slightly more natural version of Cher.

As she sat writing our supplement in triplicate, she knew full well that she was giving me a boob and thigh show - a little extra for my money.

As we crawled along at thirty-five KMH, my mind started to wander at how she passed away the long journeys; the majority sat in her little cabin alone. I figured that she was not the type who would take pleasure in reading a book.

Once the floorshow had ended, we passed the time reading, listening to music and taking pictures from the slow-moving train. At every stop, hordes more people boarded while hardly any got off.

All corridors were now jammed, and we imagined that Cher would have a small appreciative crowd in with her inside the guard's cabin.

It soon became stuffy in our compartment. Hamish made a half-hearted attempt to open the window, failed and sat down again all in one swift series of movements.

He wanted to avoid that embarrassing 'strain with all your mite' heave when the window remains closed and you assume it is locked.

So quick was his failure that the fellow passengers didn't notice and merely carried on fanning themselves.

I studied the window and thought I had worked out the opening mechanism. I would be the compartment hero. Springing into action, I opened the window with a flourish before returning to my seat.

This met with looks of approval all round, far better than the rolling eyes I would have got if the window had remained tightly shut.

There was just one issue; the window would not stay open, choosing to slowly drop into the closed position again.

It was Hamish's turn for hero status, reaching into his bag and pulling out a plastic pen. He used this to prop up the window, a pen's length obviously.

It worked a treat. Thanks once again go to Holiday Inn who had provided the prop.

The scenery was great for the return journey, rewarding me for staying awake this time.

We followed a river for a long period, which snaked through gorges and under the many bridges that we criss-crossed several times over, meaning that the river kept changing sides of the train.

The fast-flowing river was interrupted a couple of times by huge dams, but it continued its way inland for dozens of miles. We waved at fishermen and the children who splashed about excitedly in their free lido, whilst geese and heron hunted for their next meals.

As the train was so slow, we managed to get some great unblurred photos. We calculated that the average speed for the journey was a slovenly twenty-eight KMH, making Albanian trains positively speedy in comparison.

Carbuncle Bulgaria

We finally trickled into the grim Sofia suburbs and our cameras were packed away accordingly. We agreed that the four-lev supplement was the bargain of the trip, bearing in mind the discomfort that standard class would have brought. We were in our mid-forties now, so needed some comfort!

When we arrived in Sofia, we allowed the hordes to disembark first. This also had the benefit of allowing us to see Cher wiggling along the platform. Some guy was in for a good night later on we conjectured.

Ignoring the taxi driver pleas, we walked back to the hotel. VT had been a brilliant trip, probably the highlight of our Balkan tour.

That night we scrubbed up as best we could and headed for Vitosha. We ignored the same gypsy request for a cigarette, declined the 'temptation' of 'the finest lap dance in Bulgaria' and went in search of fodder.

The street was very lively that night and all restaurants seemed full. Tables had spilled out onto the road, but despite walking the entire five hundred metre length, we could not see an obvious spare seat.

As we walked back a couple left their table at an Italian. Without hesitating we were in.

The food was OK, but the Stolichno DB was right up there, served as it was in a very nice spherical glass. "I am having that," I thought, and I did. Apologies to any disapproving readers for the theft, but I am sure it wasn't missed too much.

We then went for a final beer of the trip. Again, we sat amongst some very beautiful people who were however demoted to mortal status due to their excessive smoking.

We did our usual end of trip best ofs - train journey, restaurant, city, DB, amusing moment etc., plus the equivalent worst ofs, before setting back.

We delayed our return slightly due to stopping for a nutty chocolate ice cream on the way. The gelato oddly supplemented the beer excellently.

Inevitably the gypsy girl tried once more – clearly it had been a very quiet night for her.

After we left the gypsy untempting temptress, we were to meet her elder brothers.

The three somewhat taller and bulkier Romanies appeared out of the shadows and marched towards us with noticeable menace in their manner.

We too sped up and the scene now resembled a game of chicken without cars, as we careered towards one another.

One of the trio of bronzed brats held a carrier bag and as we neared collision at warp speed, he 'accidently-on-purpose' positioned the bag towards my knee as it moved upwards in full stride.

I suddenly felt a wet sensation travel up and down my leg, quickly followed by a foul smell, a mix between sickly durian fruit, white wine vinegar, cheesy feet and stale sweat. The evil stench soon pervaded my revered walking trousers.

The fearsome threesome stopped in their tracks and started a commotion.

Whether they wanted to lambast me for causing the spillage or apologise for the mess, I do not know or care as I did not stop to ask questions, carrying on at purposeful speed away from the shrieking vagabonds with Hamish in hot pursuit.

I was too well travelled to fall for that scam. Cause a scene and offer to clean you up, but at the same time clean you out.

My mate Iain 'Ruby' Currie had once told me of a similar ruse involving dog poo on his shoe whilst he was in Rio, and luckily, I instantly remembered his words and made the connection, at least subconsciously.

Something had told me to carry on quick marching and that is exactly what I did.

Hamish was not quite sure what had happened, so I explained the equation whilst he held his nose. Whatever the vile concoction was that had spilled over me, it really did stink to high heaven. People grimaced as they passed and with very good reason.

Happily, we were by now close to our hotel and luckily this was the end of our trip for I feared it would take multiple hot washes and pints of detergent to negate the odour oozing from my trusty strides.

We skipped quickly past the dozing night receptionist, who awoke in an instant as the mobile smelling salts flitted by.

I filled the bath with hot water and poured five travel bottles of shampoo and shower gel in before tossing the tainted trousers into the bubbling cauldron.

I remembered that for some reason there was a discarded chair leg in the wardrobe and used this to stir the garment vigorously in the makeshift washing machine.

I then sprayed the room with deodorant and shut the bathroom door, leaving the putrid pants to soak.

We then recounted an incident concerning our mate Lang, a beautiful gypsy girl and her hag of a mother, whom he had encountered in Turkey with alarming consequences.

The tale is best left to the reader's imagination, but it had us roaring. Good old caravan folk, always good for a tall story! On that note, we were soon sound asleep

Next morning, I rinsed the trousers – remarkably they smelt lovely. Far better indeed than my plastic bag full of socks and boxers did anyway!

"Dovijdane Balkan Region, until the next time."

Chapter Eight - Slovenian Sojourn
(February 2017)

Thirty years after being ejected from Maribor, I finally got to Slovenia properly with a solo 48-hour long visit to Ljubljana.

Ljubljana had in fact been one of the few capital cities of Europe I hadn't visited.

Travelling on easyJet from Gatwick and staying for two nights in an Airbnb room in a central flat for a total cost of £110, made it almost rude not to go.

Fleeced

Wary of solo trips that I made in 2016 to Riga & Bratislava, I decided that I would invest in a taxi, especially as I arrived after dark and would be staying in a residential area.

On those previous occasions I had wandered pretty aimlessly for over an hour in search of accommodation, having been dropped at the closest bus stop.

My appalling map reading skills (never that easy in the dark), combined with my reluctance to ask anybody, invariably get me lost.

However, you will be aware that I am also very wary of rip-off taxi drivers. The night-time taxi rank at Ljubljana Airport seemed to be a haphazard affair. No taxi attendant pointing you to your wheels and no obvious vehicle queue that you just walk to the front of.

I therefore decided to choose the driver that was least likely to fleece me. I chose an elderly lady driver.

The wizened chauffeur then proceeded to con me royally, not only taking a circuitous route to my destination, but also having a meter whose numbers spun so fast that I grew dizzy watching them.

Naturally she spoke zero English, making any conversation about extortion totally pointless. Some judge of character I turned out to be!

I also wasn't entirely sure we were in the right place. There were no street lights and it was pitch black, being 9.30PM. The female felon pointed me roughly in the apparent right direction.

Walking past three blocks of flats, happily security lights flashed on to confirm that I was indeed in the right vicinity.

My accommodation was in apartment block four and I rang the bell as instructed. Thankfully, my host Miha answered and buzzed me in, telling me to take the elevator to the fourth floor.

Miha welcomed me to his country and confirmed that the taxi lady had indeed seen me coming. He was to arrange a taxi back on the Sunday with a mate of his for less than half what I had been charged to get there.

He lived in the three-bedroom apartment with his mother. It was only five-minutes-walk to the centre and armed with easy to follow directions, I left for a quick falafel, a couple of splendid dark beers (Laško Zlatorog) and some atmospheric night shots of the bridges over the River Ljubljanica.

Slovenian Graffiti

I was up bright and early for breakfast supplied by my generous host. First up I had to work out the shower that had multiple taps and jets pointing in all directions.

Predictably I got the controls hopelessly wrong, blasting myself with freezing cold water and soaking the small bathroom in the process. At least it knocked any sleepiness out of my system!

Miha was to join me in the kitchen for a chat after I had showered and wiped up the bathroom.

He was a young child in 1991 when Slovenia gained independence from Yugoslavia and although he remembered nothing of the ten-day war with the Serb dominated Yugoslav army, he was fiercely patriotic and extremely proud of his city.

I recounted my infamous story about my first visit to Slovenia and confirmed that I had no intention of venturing back to Maribor.

My first port of call was Old Rog, an old bicycle factory turned Bohemian squat. There are a few similar such places in Ljubljana and suffice to say they divide opinion with some believing they are artistic expressions of a free society, whilst others argue that they are a blight to make your eyes sore.

I quite enjoyed my saunter around the graffiti, rusting metal and creative objects. I may have felt differently if I lived in the city, I suppose.

Ljubljana is well known for its bridges, the first of which I crossed being the Dragon's Bridge.

Legend has it that a dragon used to live in the river, possibly due to vapor rising on a hot day resembling dragon smoke. The dragon is now the symbol of the city and every year there is a dragon carnival with appropriately themed fancy-dress and floats.

Whatever the truth of the legend, the two snarling dragons at either end made for an imposing sight.

The cobbled thoroughfares alongside the river are stuffed nowadays with bars & restaurants, whilst there are several novel statues of various creatures such as skeletal dogs, a brood of ducks, fang baring piranhas & giant frogs, to catch the eye.

Before long I came to the next bridge known as Butcher's Bridge. This is the one that has had the lovers padlock treatment, which people seem to either love or hate. I actually quite like them as they do make for some interesting shots in the sunlight.

I soon then come to the unique Triple Bridge. The Triple Bridge with its 642 balusters, is a group of three bridges connecting the historical medieval town on one bank and the modern city on the other. In truth the structure itself is made from rather bland materials, but the unusual design more than makes up for that.

History Lesson

It was now time for me to stop at tourist information and join the Jože Plečnik tour that I had pre-booked whilst sat at Gatwick Airport.

It turned out that this would be a very private tour as I was the only punter!

Mario my guide was extremely knowledgeable, not only about Slovenia, Ljubljana and Plečnik, but also world affairs as a whole, with BREXIT especially being a well discussed topic.

He gave me some more detail regarding the ten-day conflict that followed the Slovenian declaration of independence on 25 June 1991.

It was fought between the Slovenian Territorial Defence and the Yugoslav People's Army, lasting from 27 June until 7 July 1991. History now states that it officially marked the beginning of the Yugoslav Wars.

As well as designing his capital city, Plečnik is also attributed with planning much of modern-day Prague and you can definitely see a lot of similarities. He is to Ljubljana what Gaudí is to Barcelona and is considered a national hero.

We took the funicular up to Ljubljana Castle for some splendid views and then walked down the other side to a far quieter part of the city away from the main touristic parts.

The castle had seen plenty of action over the years due to the city's strategically important position, with battles involving the Venetians, Ottomans, Serbs & Habsburgs amongst others.

We ended in Plečnik' s house, all pretty much left as it has been at the time of his death in 1957.

We then had that awkward moment when Mario was clearly expecting a tip for his excellent tour wisdom, but I knew that I only had a €50 note on me. He was good, but not that good!

I restored honour later that day by leaving €10 in an envelope back at the tourist information office.

After the two-hour tour, I wandered around the compact city taking in plenty of scenic spots. This included the notable 13th Century Cobbler's Bridge, the latest version of which had been designed by Plečnik.

The open-air fruit & veg market was great and provided a cheap and healthy lunch. There was also a colourful flower section, though the sellers didn't seem to be doing much of a trade going by their grumpy faces.

That evening after a tasty inexpensive meal, I found a rock club for some thrash metal entertainment. Not my favourite music, but with a lively crowd and a couple of beers it was highly enjoyable.

It happened to the birthday of the lead singer (shouter more like) and he was presented with a bottle of Jack Daniels. In true rock & roll fashion, he took a mighty swig from the bottle, before it was passed around the bar for everybody to take their own swig.

I politely declined, on health grounds rather than any particular dislike for Jack.

Training Day

I had decided that I would do a side trip from Ljubljana and having dismissed the idea of Maribor for old time's sake and deciding that Lake Bled was too far considering that I would be flying home that same day, it needed to be somewhere close by.

I therefore plumped for a train journey to the town of Skofja Loka in Upper Carniola, with its riverside location, imposing castle and renowned museum.

The train took thirty minutes to do the 20km. I had figured that I had a good four hours there before having to venture back to the Slovenian capital.

We were soon out in the sticks and in no time, I was alighting at Skofja's remote station.

The day was Sunday and although there was allegedly a bus, I eventually decided that I would walk the gently ascending 3km uphill into town. As no bus passed me en route, I for once felt vindicated by my decision.

The air had an alpine feel and the walk was both invigorating and picturesque as I was surrounded by evergreens in the hills to my left and neat homesteads to my right.

As I approached the outskirts of the town, the Selca Sora river reared its picturesque head. I lingered for ten minutes basking in the sunshine on a wooden bridge taking in the babbling water and the realisation filtered through that I was feeling very peaceful indeed.

I then continued the climb into town, past the church and into the main mediaeval streets, soon finding myself sat in the main square enjoying coffee & cake.

Texting Mrs Wilbur and wishing she was with me, I had my second and third realisation of the morning – that I was so lucky to be able to travel on a whim and that I had a very understanding wife.

My thoughts were broken by the midday bells, stirring me into life for the culmination of my ascent up to the castle.

The castle itself was shut for the winter, but the mooch around the grounds was very pleasant indeed. There were ancient buildings to peer into and a marvellous view of the town, the valley and Skofja's second river, Poljane Sora.

The best was yet to come. The castle museum was an absolute gem, housed over two floors within the castle complex.

It covered over a millennia of Skofja Loka history with one floor dedicated to art and the second to the ethnology of the region.

The art section contained famous Slovenian paintings from the 17th Century onwards and other objects such as furniture that were well worthy of attention, plus rooms laid out as they would have been a couple of centuries before.

It was however the ethnological collection that I loved, most especially the ancient farming equipment that evoked images of Jethro Tull and his famous seed drill.

There were plenty of other artisan pieces such as printing presses, spinning wheels and distillery equipment.

It was like I had landed in the UK's pre-Industrial Revolution era of the cottage industries of Northern England with its 'spinning jenny' weaving machines.

There was also a very well stocked armoury and an unusual (some may say distasteful) collection of stuffed mammals. Taxidermy apart, this was one of my favourite ever museums and a real bargain at €5. I was also the only visitor that afternoon – the joys of out of season travel!

So good was my visit in fact that I completely lost track of time, necessitating a speed walk of Olympic proportions to arrive at the station two minutes before my train departed. I was then thankful that I was alone as I could never have put Mrs Wilbur through that!

If you ever get to Ljubljana, I thoroughly recommend a trip to Skofja Loka. If you travel by bus you get right to the centre in thirty-minutes, which may be a tad easier on the knees!

There was just time for a farewell DB near the Dragon Bridge, before I contentedly set off for the airport.

Chapter Nine – Many Happy Returns
(September 2017)

After an absence of five years, Hamish and I decided that we should make a joint return to the Balkans.

Our trip would start in the popular Greek holiday island of Corfu, before we would take a short ferry ride to Albania, followed by a bus journey up the spine of the country to our old friend Tirana, another couple of road jaunts to the Kosovo cities of Prizren & Pristina, train travels to Skopje & Belgrade and finally another train to Timisoara in Romania.

Rendezvous

Hamish had flown to Corfu from Bristol, meaning he arrived six hours before my London Gatwick flight. This gave him time to explore the island's historic forts and atmospheric old town, which I had visited a couple of years before with Mrs Wilbur.

It seemed that I was the only easyJet passenger en route to the Greek Island who would not be staying for a week or two's sea & sunshine. The word around me was focusing on best beaches, best full English and biggest issues (no full English being available seemingly the biggest fear vexing the sunseekers).

Whilst an extended period in Corfu certainly has its huge benefits (Mrs Wilbur and I had spent a splendid week there), I was a traveller on this trip. Admittedly I would start and end as a relaxed tourist, but in between there was overland travelling to enjoy.

Despite the September day being baking hot and the island having several very nice DBs brewed locally, Hamish decided he should wait to savour his first beer until he could enjoy it with me.

By the time I arrived at 11pm, my pal was therefore spitting feathers.

I met him at a central point and hardly had time to say hello before we were marching to a very pleasant bar that he had located earlier. I had my rucksack with me of course, but this did not stop me moving swiftly as I too was very keen for dark refreshment.

The unimaginatively named Corfu Beer Dark Ale was rather lovely. So much so that after a mere five minutes we were ordering a second.

I may have mentioned before that my sense of direction is woeful and maybe the only person in the world who is worse than me would be Hamish. Anybody who knows Corfu Town will know that it is another labyrinth like old town, rather like Split.

Throw in two rapidly consumed 5% DBs, a dose of tiredness and a complete inability to read maps, and you are left with "our flat is just around the corner," becoming a desperate forty-minute search for our sleeping quarters.

We were staying in an Airbnb apartment situated alongside an ancient Venetian well, and after a circuitous route there was a feeling of almighty relief when said well revealed itself after we turned a blind corner.

Our flat was on the basic side, but its beds were comfortable enough and quite frankly were all that we needed at that particular moment.

Our first mission next morning was to secure our flying dolphin tickets for the following day to the Albanian town of Sarandë.

Having travelled by ferry to Corfu from the Greek mainland a couple of years previously, I knew where we needed to head to get to the ferry port where the ticket vendors were located.

Tickets were quickly secured. Hamish enquired of me whether we should ask where the vessel left from. My male 'I know everything' ego took over and I replied that I knew exactly where the departure would be from. Mmmmmm.

We spent the rest of the day chilling in the lovely late Summer sunshine. I visited the famed Church of St Spyridon on my own, whilst Hamish hunted our boggle-eyed toys. Built in the 14th Century, the church houses the blackened remains of feted St Spyridon and I had arrived on one of the special days when they open the casket that they are kept in.

I therefore queued with the pilgrims, who unlike me knew exactly who they were going to see, for a peek at the black mummified body dressed in colourful robes. Rather creepy looking if you ask me but I was certainly in a minority of about one.

Afterwards I met up with Hamish once more to locate a tiny ocean side chapel built into a cliff that I had stumbled across with Mrs Wilbur on my previous visit. All that walking was thirsty work, necessitating a couple of DBs and some fresh calamari sat by the Ionian with a view up to the old fort.

A Short Crossing

Next morning, we left in plenty of time to get to the 9 o'clock ferry to Albania. It was not far to walk and after 15 minutes the ferry building honed into view. We arrived at 8.30 but I was slightly concerned that the place seemed deserted.

I had only gone and done it again. I had brought us to the domestic terminal with the international departure point being a pink building that we could just about make out in the distance, further around the crescent-shaped harbour.

With no sign of any taxi in the vicinity we set off on a route march, eventually getting through passport control and security with three-minutes to spare.

We were as you can imagine hot, sweaty and stressed. I certainly would not be so cock-sure for the rest of the trip, whilst Hamish was reminded not to trust my assertions in the future.

Happily, for Hamish in particular, the sea was millpond smooth and the thirty-minute passage passed without any sickness issues.

Although we had left at 9, we actually arrived at 8.30 due to Albania being on a different time zone to their neighbours.

In a slice of good fortune, we had arrived at our sea view hotel (Hotel Titania) in time for breakfast and for €2.50 a head we were soon gorging on cereals, fruit, yoghurt, bread & cheese and endless supplies of coffee.

All of this sat on a very pleasant open-air terrace overlooking the ocean. If this location had been on the French Riviera it would have cost a fortune rather than the €45 per night that we paid. Memories of our earlier harassed yomp in search of our departure point therefore soon faded away into the ether.

Popping downstairs to ask at reception about a couple of excursions we wanted to do, I was surprised and delighted to be met with, "Aah, Pitkin!"

My Norman Wisdom t-shirt had at last struck gold in Albania. I had the receptionist chortling away as he recalled his childhood times when all the family would huddle around a small black & white TV to watch films featuring the British comic.

During the oppressive Hoxha years, the farcical capers of our Norman was one of the few foreign films allowed by the strict censors. As much of the humour was visual in a similar way to Benny Hill and Mr Bean, any language barrier did not matter.

I suspect however that the dialogue was dubbed into Albanian, no doubt with a rather different script to the original version, so as to make it even more politically correct or perhaps to serve Albanian propaganda.

We made our plans – that afternoon we would pay a visit to 'Blue Eye', with a trip to the Roman ruins at Butrint saved for the following day.

Sarandë itself seemed a very pleasant place, unsurprisingly very similar in appearance to nearby Greece. We would have plenty of time to explore as we would be staying for two nights.

We could have taken a bus close to the natural blue pool & spring known as Blue Eye (Syri i kaltër to give its official name) costing only 40 Lek (€0.25), but thankfully in those wealthier days we had enough money to avoid the hot & stuffy public vehicle in favour of a taxi costing €20.

Despite being only 22km from Sarandë, it took us an hour to get there due to the poor, winding road, with the last 2km being off-road entirely and extremely bumpy. The entrance fee was €1, free if you were a goat, many of whom had arrived well before us.

The pool itself was beautiful. Nobody knows why it is so deep blue, neither do they know exactly how deep it is (certainly over 50 metres apparently). The dark blue centre is surrounded by lighter turquoise, very much resembling a blue eye.

I thoughtfully reminded Hamish of his aborted attempt to see the wonderful Blue Lagoon on the Italian island of Capri in 2001. He got seasick as our small boat bobbed about as we awaited our transfer to a rowing boat to take us into the cave.

He was virtually carried onto a row boat with his then girlfriend, and instead of visiting the lagoon they made straight for the shore where Hamish laid in starfish position for the best part of an hour.

At Blue Eye a viewing platform had been built suspended above the river, to give you a bird's eye view of the colourful waters.

Frustratingly we had to wait twenty-minutes for our turn behind a wedding party intent on a full-on photo-shoot of the whole party with the bride & groom in full marriage garb, before we could walk up the roughly hewn steps to the platform.

We lingered at the spot for a total of thirty-minutes, quite frankly plenty of time to take in the natural phenomena. We could have given it a miss quite honestly, and figured the two-hour round trip was only just about worth the effort.

Far more pleasing for us was watching the sunset back in Sarandë with an ice-cold Korça. We were clearly in a resort popular with Albanian families, with plenty of kiosks selling toys, sunhats, sunglasses, swimwear and a huge choice of candies & ice creams.

We watched dozens of families and couples strolling along the promenade as we sipped our DB. Despite the fact that the sun was fast slipping behind the horizon, the sunhat seller in particular seemed to be doing a brisk trade.

We chose a nice fish restaurant to eat in that evening. We were initially disappointed to be told that there was no beer available due to the refrigerator not working. However, a waiter was soon dispatched and five-minutes later he returned with his (our) bounty of a couple of cold Korças.

The restaurant more than lived up to its #2 rating on Trip Adviser. Fresh fish at reasonable prices, plus a willingness to go and get us two more DBs after we polished off the first two in double-quick time.

In Ruins

Before negotiating a taxi for our journey to Butrint next morning, we went to the bus ticket office to enquire about the minibus to Tirana for the next day.

We had hoped to only have to bus it part of the way northwards along the coast to Vlore and to then take a train to Durres and from there onto Tirana.

It did not matter a jot that this would probably take hours at an average speed of less than 40 kmh. The thrill of being on a foreign train far outweighed the need for speed.

Sadly though, Albania's train network was in disarray with no trains operational in the whole country. This was due to an alleged multi-million-euro upgrade programme that had no sign of getting very far.

At the time of writing (February 2019) there is one train a day taking five hours from Vlore to Tirana, however this departs at the not so convenient time of 05.40. Clearly the time must work for some.

So, bus it would have to be for the entire journey. There were six morning buses to choose from and we favoured the 09.30 that would take seven hours to get to the capital.

We were emphatically told by the walnut-faced Albanian dude that there was no need to pre-book a ticket and that we should merely turn up around nine next day.

Having turned down two taxi drivers who sniffed a rip-off pay day, we settled on our third attempt at negotiation and a fare of €25 for the round trip to and from Butrint, plus as much waiting time as we wanted.

The road was a whole lot better than the Blue Eye route, but still took 40-minutes to travel less than 20km. This was mainly due to the large queue of traffic that approached the ancient city via a narrow road.

Butrint had initially been a Greek settlement, later to become Roman.

There is evidence that the city (Bouthroton in ancient times) was first settled in the 10th to 8th Century BC, but it wasn't until the 4th Century BC that it came to prominence due to its strategic coastal location, proximity to Corfu and its natural inland haven for ships provided by Lake Butrint.

A good two-hours was spent ambling amongst the ruins of the UNESCO World Heritage Site, that was almost completely surrounded by the waters of the sea and the lake.

The well-preserved amphitheatre was the highlight, but there were many more buildings & columns worthy of note. However, having visited far superior sights in the Middle East, it was hard to get too excited.

Back in Sarandë by early afternoon, we strolled around the natural harbour for as far as the eye could see. A there and back walk that took us two hours to complete in 20-degree heat, more than enough effort to warrant a DB.

The evening was completed with a very nice pizza and chilled DBs consumed on the hotel terrace overlooking the twinkling lights of street lamps, boats & buildings, that shone out over the ink-black waters.

The Never-Ending Journey

Next morning, we turned up at nine as recommended. We were treated to a cheery hello. "I save you last two tickets." The elderly vendor smiled through stained teeth as he proffered the pieces of paper in our direction.

What he had not informed us was that the seats were right in the back row in the corner of the cramped minibus. This did not auger well for a seven-hour ride.

As we reached the Sarandë suburbs, the already full van picked up four more passengers who sat in the aisle.

Just to make matters worse, our journey was to remain inland, meaning we were trailing up and down mountains on very poor stony roads that twisted and turned like a 'twisty turny thing' (acknowledgements to Blackadder – I would have likened it to being like a teabag in a hurricane myself!).

Hamish is not a good traveller at the best of times. He had to summon all his will-power to agree to the crossing from Corfu and he had taken a sea-sickness tablet ahead of our journey north. Unfortunately, this would not save him.

Forty-five minutes in, he turned a shade of green as we were jerked & twisted in our seats, this being despite the fact that we were pretty much wedged in between the window, the seat in front and a rather large passenger to my left.

It was all too much for my travel buddy, who announced in a pained voice that there was "no way that he could stomach this for seven hours".

This was a call to action for me. I had noticed that the girl sat in the aisle at the front of the bus had an American accent. Hamish confirmed that he would happily swap seats with her, so I made the difficult journey up to her to ask whether she would mind.

This tested my ungainly balancing skills to the maximum as I squeezed past those in the aisle, with the bus lurching aggressively from side to side.

How I did not end up in a fellow passenger's lap, like I had done eleven years before in Ohrid, was a minor miracle.

It was a tad embarrassing approaching the girl to explain my pal's plight and to ask her to come to the back to be wedged in next to me, but gladly Beth was very understanding and readily agreed.

It was arranged that I would go to tell Hamish whilst Beth remained in her position, lest a fellow aisle dweller take a liking to her 'prime spot' and claim it for themselves.

Cue much shuffling back and forwards, feet trampled upon and awkward embraces with passengers as the three of us fought to stay upright on our separate journeys. We were the only non-Albanians aboard and easily the least popular!

Incredibly, ten-minutes later we stopped for a fag break and everybody exited the bus. Everybody that is except for Hamish who stayed in his perch like a limpet.

There was no way he was chancing losing his hard-won position. This meant he was in everybody else's way of course, with a fair amount of displeasure pointed in his direction.

Despite the frequent cigarette breaks, we seemed to be making fairly good progress as we were now on far better roads with us having completed the mountainous part of the journey.

We arrived on the outskirts of the city of Fier in around four hours, having travelled 163km of the 280km journey. With the highway ahead of us appearing good, we were overjoyed to think that we might actually be ahead of schedule, seeing as we were now well over half-way to Tirana.

The bus was still full and pretty uncomfortable. At least I had been given the chance of a nice chat with Beth. This probably saved the journey from being ranking as badly as my two worst ever such European journeys – an overnighter from Odessa to Sevastopol and the worst of the lot from Erzurum in Turkey to the border with Georgia on the Black Sea.

Nowhere near as bad as my 1998 journey from Na Trang to Hoi An in Vietnam mind! I will definitely write up the European hell rides for a future book, and maybe the Asian one too one day.

Beth worked for an American mining & construction company in the Human Resources department. They had an office in Tirana, which required an annual visit from the Head Office HR. Beth had been chosen to travel on this occasion and had therefore decided to take some time off to explore some of Albania.

We swapped travel stories and aspirations, instantly transporting us both to more pleasant climes than a cramped & stuffy minibus. Beth was definitely chipped from the same block as me – I have amalgamated countless leisure breaks with work trips overseas as well.

When we got to a coastal city called Kavaje, there was some light relief at last. Half the bus got off and only a couple more got on, meaning there would now be plenty of space to stretch out in.

This was also the stopping off point for Beth. One of her colleagues lived there and Beth would be staying the night before heading for Tirana next day.

We were only 53km away from the capital and were confident that we would arrive an hour early. Sadly, we were very mistaken. 10km from central Tirana we encountered gridlock. The 8km to Tirana's main ramshackle bus station was to take us ninety excruciating minutes.

We could have walked it quicker, though by the look of the polluting vehicles that surrounded us, I am pretty sure we would have perished from asphyxiation before we arrived.

It took a good ten minutes to shake off the effects of a rather tortuous journey, and just as long to evade the throng of pushy taxi drivers that greeted us. A baying mob of chain-smoking scruffs, desperate for a few lek or better still, euros or dollars.

We tramped towards the main road down the same rocky, puddle-strewn path that our bus had just driven down. A rather timid looking chap then enquired whether we required a taxi. He seemed harmless and in desperate need of some custom, so we agreed a €5 fee to take us to our hotel.

He led us down a small alley to our taxi. When I say taxi, I mean in the loosest sense of the word. Not only was the vehicle certainly not a taxi, but looked barely drivable too. The ancient Lada had more duct tape holding bits together than I had ever seen before, the tyres were worn, the windscreen cracked, whilst there was as much rust as yellow bodywork in evidence.

Hamish looked at me and rather than recoiling in horror at the sight of our chariot in waiting, we both just grinned. How Albanian!

Somehow our driver got through the traffic and eventually found our hotel after several abortive attempts. Unsurprisingly he now wanted €10, but seemed pleased enough with six.

Fair & Square

After a short rest that enabled the world to stop spinning in Hamish's head, we set off to explore. We had visited Tirana ten years before of course, so how much had it changed?

It took us fifteen minutes to find out. We approached the hub of the city that is Skanderbeg Square, the place where I had been injured a decade before by a small boy riding a toy car.

Instead of a potholed roundabout, non-functioning fountains and a haven for those less fortunate to hang-out, we found a huge pedestrianised marble square with an underground car park below it.

The museum, mosque, clocktower, opera house, international hotel, statue of Skanderbeg on horseback and municipal buildings still remained, but the character of the area had been completely changed, its soul flattened by planners.

We also found evidence of more construction taking place that would alter the landscape even more.

The square was in fact all fenced off due to famed Albanian violinist Shkelzen Doli giving an open-air concert that night.

We were therefore unable to even walk on the former roundabout, but at least had the compensation later on of peering through a gap in the fence to take in some of the fine virtuoso performance.

After procuring bus tickets for the next day's journey to Kosovo, we returned to our comfortable hotel for a shower and rest.

That evening we went in search of the Buda Bar that we had enjoyed so much ten years previously. I roughly remembered the area where the bar had stood on its own in a residential area.

Well, we could not find Buda, but there were now dozens of bars, clubs & restaurants in the vicinity. 32 years after the repressive dictator Enver Hoxha, the city was taking off and the younger generation were now extremely well catered for.

We savoured some wonderful Korça and a vegetarian pizza. We did however have the laughable episode of one pizza arriving covered in ham that we sent back. Almost inevitably a 'new' one arrived a few minutes later, with the marks of where the ham had been removed clear to see! Third time lucky thankfully.

Men with a Mission

Next morning, we returned to the square in the vain hope that Tiger Man may be there photographing kids alongside his striped toy.

Sadly, the developers had flattened his entrepreneurialism too. We lambasted ourselves once more for not having our photograph taken when we had the opportunity.

Our mission that day was threefold – to visit Enver Hoxha's former nuclear bunker, to take a cable car up into the mountains that surround Tirana and to catch the bus to Prizren. A lot to cram in, especially as our bus was leaving at 3pm.

We had therefore set off at eight, leaving our bags at the hotel for collection later. The bus to the bunker, now a museum called BunkArt, left from behind the clock tower.

We didn't have to wait long for our bus to depart for the €0.25 journey and twenty-minutes later we were dropped off a short walk from the museum.

To get to the attraction, we had to walk through some large gates and down a long tunnel that sloped gradually downwards. The tunnel would have been sealed off to the outside world in the event of a nuclear or chemical attack, enabling the privileged few to survive as the masses perished.

The €3 entrance was an absolute bargain. In a similar way to the nuclear submarine base we had visited in Balaklava, Crimea a few years before, this was a unique experience, no fragments of pots and coins shown there.

We walked through some corridors to our first port of call – Hoxha's living quarters, unsurprisingly the largest in the bunker. They consisted of entrance lobby, living room, office, bedroom & bathroom. It was furnished as it would have been in the '70s with the TV & radio tuned to propaganda speeches and military parades.

The windowless rooms were threadbare, simply decorated, but well lit. You could even pick up the telephone to hear Hoxha barking orders down the other end.

The rest of the place was equally enthralling. Corridors that twisted maze like, metal staircases leading you further below the surface, the loud speaker system crackling into life as it would have done as a primary source of communication.

The information relayed to us was to be careful on the stairways and to visit the museum shop before leaving.

Many of the rooms that used to house living quarters, signal offices, kitchens, surgeries and the like, had now been adapted to house exhibits, photographs, military equipment etc.

One had been done up in the typical style of a '70s living room, minimalist and with radio again tuned to propaganda, plus the mandated portrait of Hoxha hanging over the fireplace. It reminded me of George Orwell's 1984, but happily there was no Room 101.

One room housed photographs of post war Tirana being visited by the British forces. Dame Vera Lynn blasted out of the speakers, an unexpected reminder of home.

Another room was pitch black so that you could shut the door and imagine what the windowless bunker would have been like if electricity had failed or been rationed.

BunkArt is rated number one attraction in Tirana and for very good reason. A fabulous experience. BunkArt2 has now been opened in a separate bunker elsewhere in the city. I will visit should I ever be in Tirana a third time.

Nearby was the other of Tirana's top attractions that we would take in, a cable car taking you high up into the mountains.

The ride lasted 15 minutes each way for what was described as the longest such ride in the Balkans. A round trip was €5 and as we just about had sufficient time, off we trotted up the hill to the base station.

The views were superb as we glided high above the treetops & farms. There were restaurants and a hotel up top, as well as very attractive hiking trails through a national park.

We just had a few minutes to take in the view of the capital below however, before ascending again.

We did start to fret for a few minutes when we failed to find a taxi with less than an hour to go to our bus to Prizren.

Luckily however, a bus showed after five minutes, giving us time to retrieve our bags from the hotel, buy a nutritious bus lunch of Doritos and coke, and even to purchase a take away coffee from the University of Albania (aka UFO) cafe.

Our Metropolitain bus pulled up ten minutes late as it happened, but thankfully was only a third full, thus giving us plenty of room to stretch out and contemplate our second visit to Kosovo.

Uneasy Truce

As you are aware, relations between Serbia and Kosovo have remained very strained, with the Serb nation never accepting that Kosovo was not part of their motherland.

What had appeared to be an act of reconciliation had recently gone very pear-shaped indeed.

In January 2017, following years of negotiation, the Kosovar authorities allowed limited passenger trains to start again from Belgrade to the Serb majority city of Mitrovica based in the north of Kosovo. It was to be a landmark route as the tracks had remained silent for over two decades.

However, the train only made it as far as Raška, the final railway station before crossing Kosovo's national borders. The Kosovar authorities had gotten wind of the fact that the train was liveried in Serbian nationalistic slogans proclaiming Kosovo as Serbian.

They then sent police and military to Raška to halt the provocative train's progress.

There then followed a war of words with the Serbian authorities accusing the Kosovars of setting landmines further along the tracks to blow up the train, with Kosovo countering that Serbia had violated international law with its nationalistic posturing and threat of reprisals.

Eventually the passengers were allowed to continue by bus and the train returned to Belgrade. It had all been a huge publicity stunt by Serbian Prime Minister Aleksandar Vučić & President

Tomislav Nikolić, to gain greater popularity at home. It worked as they were both re-elected soon afterwards.

Tensions between the nations had however been ratcheted up considerably – so much so that travel advice to UK citizens was to only travel there if unavoidable. That had never stopped us before……

What we had found out was that it was not possible to enter Serbia directly from Kosovo. This would mean that we would have to take a train from Pristina to Skopje and to travel onto Belgrade from there.

Our journey to Prizren was to be just a three-hour ride on the Albania-Kosovo Highway (the Autostrada Shqipëri-Kosovë), a wonderful piece of engineering that has more than halved the former nine-hour journey time from the Albanian capital to the Kosovan one.

The four-lane road cost around €1 billion to complete and cuts a swathe through pine forests and mountains, with us traversing through a near six-kilometre long tunnel at one point.

It was also a picturesque journey past the odd Albanian bunker, through villages and past farms with fields of curly kale & cabbage. For a few kilometers were travelled alongside a snaking river, switching back and forth over it via several viaducts.

Passport Palpitations

Just before border control, the bus ticket inspector collected up our passports & identity cards to be handed over to the disinterested looking policemen sat in their cabin between the lanes of traffic.

He flicked through the pile, giving the odd glance through the bus windows. Hamish & I were the only people on board with zero Albanian in our genetic make-up, so seemed to receive more scrutiny than most.

We must have passed inspection as the large wad of documents were soon passed back and we were waved on our way.

The bus man then proceeded to call out the passport/ID card names, so that the rightful owner could be reunited with their right to travel.

I pretended not to be concerned when we were down to the last passport and my name was yet to be called.

Concern rose however when the name called out did not belong to me!

I was sat in row eight and moved uneasily up to the front of the bus to enquire as to the whereabouts of my passport. I was met with incredulous surprise, "I gave it back to you, I am sure."

I had reached my patience limit, "no you did not, you must still have it!!?"

I was asked to write my name down, not an easy thing to do when your stress levels are at fever pitch and the bus is travelling at 100 kmh. The bus attendant screwed his eyes up at my name. He then shouted something out in Albanian. I got the 'Weelyarm

Leenstell' part and figured he was asking my fellow travellers whether anybody had my passport by mistake.

It took only a few seconds to confirm that nobody did. How could they have lost my passport? I assumed that it was back at the border post and requested (I mean forcibly demanded) that we turn around and go back.

I was informed that the next turning opportunity was 15 km away. I could tell that they were very reluctant to make an unscheduled stop as it would have made the bus probably an hour late in reaching its final destination of Pristina.

After searching the floor of the bus around the front seats, the attendant made a phone call, presumably to his boss. The conversation fell silent at our end and you could tell by his expression that employee was getting a right ear-bashing from employer.

The barking down the line probably went along the lines of "How could you allow this to happen, this will cost me over €100, not to mention the inconvenience to my loyal passengers, actually it will cost you over €100 as you can pay for your mistake."

To be quite honest I did not really care less as my stomach was in knots, sick with concern. The one thing that you should never lose whilst travelling is your passport.

Memories of the hassle we went through thirty-years previous when Poll lost his passport in Munich came flooding back.

I was of course totally blameless in all of this, yet it would be me stuck in Albania or Kosovo trying to get an emergency replacement, our entire trip possibly ruined and all future bookings forfeit.

That was if there was indeed a UK embassy in Tirana or Pristina*. I trusted that there would be and Hamish guaranteed as much. Neither of us could be 100% sure in reality.

We pulled off the highway, but instead of turning around to go back to the border, we parked up at a small service station to allow the hapless attendant to go and make another call, this time using a payphone. I presumed he was trying to call the border guard box.

Almost the entire bus saw this as a cigarette break opportunity and made a beeline for the exits. The obese, perspiring driver thought he might as well do likewise, so wheezily levered himself up from his seat.

I also decided that I needed some air to decompress from all of the stress that I was feeling. As I moved forward, something caught my eye on the driver's seat. There lay a slightly creased, burgundy coloured document. My passport!

It must have slipped out of the pile when the border guards handed them back through the window and somehow ended up being sandwiched between ample buttocks and seat.

I was overjoyed of course but resisted the temptation to triumphantly kiss my retrieved documentation having realised just in time where it had rested for the past half-hour!

240

Hamish beamed with relief, whilst I dutifully ran after the bus attendant to impart the good news.

Two blasts on the bus's horn signalled we would be on our way again. The bus soon filled up again and we were off.

Our bus was bound for Pristina and we stopped just outside Prizren to transfer to a minibus for the short ride into the town that was familiar to us from ten years previous.

We had an unusual check-in with the reception desk on the edge of a building site as the hotel was under renovation. The staff could not apologise enough. The rooms were absolutely fine though, if on the spartan side.

Kosovo's second city straddles the River Bistrica and is easily small enough to explore by foot. We had a quick look before nightfall and witnessed the atmospheric call to prayer.

We stood by the main mosque which started the cacophony, before it was joined by up to forty others around the city in making an eerie, almost unworldly, noise.

It started to rain that night and was destined not to stop until we left Kosovo.

The damp conditions had no effect on our spirits though as next morning we yomped up once more to the castle for some splendid views, revisited the simple but impressive mosque and just meandered around the laid back centre with its plethora of cafes & bars.

We were pleased to see that the small city had hardly changed at all. Progress is definitely not always for the better in my opinion.

Despite the constant drizzle we enjoyed our visit but were also very happy to catch the early morning bus to bustling Pristina after two nights of peace & quiet.

We had hoped to take some train trips from Pristina having found a train map on the internet. However, this particular map was well past its sell by date as no trains were in operation.

Early next morning, we stood by the main bridge as instructed by the receptionist and sure enough, after a seven-minute wait the bus arrived and stopped as we requested by waving our arms furiously in the air. A new capital city beckoned.

* ***We subsequently discovered that there were UK embassies in both Tirana & Pristina. Why we never check these things before we travel, I do not know.***

Proud Pristina

The journey took a shade under two hours and our subsequent taxi had us at our hotel by ten. We had purposely booked a hotel close to the train station as we intended to leave on the 07.10 departure to Skopje the next day.

The hotel's website blurb had claimed to be just 200 metres from our departure point, but what it failed to mention was that this was though a trading estate, across a wasteland, down a muddy bank and over the train lines.

This was to be our first port of call as we needed to check the trains were still definitely running. Predictably I slipped on the muddy bank, drawing blood from my wrist & knee and collecting a large swathe of mud on to my trousers and jacket.

I looked quite the tramp entering the scruffy, rundown, pink-painted station, which showed very little sign of life. However, a timetable seemed to confirm out train to Skopje did indeed leave daily shortly after seven.

As we looked around for a loo that would allow me to clean up a little, the station manager/guard/signalman/cleaner popped out from inside his office.

Despite the language barrier, he managed to confirm that our train would run and that we did not need to buy tickets beforehand. He also took pity on my sorry state, leading me into his office to hand me some wet wipes and point me to his own personal bathroom. What a lovely guy.

As it was still rather inclement and my knee & wrist were still smarting, we decided to invest in the luxury of a taxi to take us to the Ethnographic Museum (Muzeu Etnologjik) which was actually a traditional Kosovar house furnished as it would have been for centuries.

Amil, our enthusiastic guide, told us the history of the Ottoman style dwelling, as well as much of the recent torrid history of the fledgling nation.

He was just eleven years-old when the conflict finished and he told us stories of corpses in the road, hunger and constant fear.

He also gave us some good tourist information advice, all in all well worth the €10 tip, especially as entry to the museum had been free.

There followed a quick march through the thriving fruit 'n veg market and after a few wrong turns we came to the small (and rather unexciting) mosque that Amil had told us about.

It was now lunch time and we had been recommended to try flia, the local favourite made up of 15-20 pancake like layers with not much in between as it happened. It was supposed to contain cinnamon paste, sour cream or something similar, but all we could see and taste was grease!

After one mouthful for me and an aborted mouthful from Hamish, we abandoned the 'delicacy' for delicious chocolate cake and strong coffee. Make that two cakes!

We then made our way along George Bush Boulevard (Bulevardi XHORXH BUSH) to the ultra-modern Mother Teresa cathedral, which had only been consecrated two weeks before our visit.

George was of course a national hero in both Albania & Kosovo for supporting the Kosovar independence bid. Dubya may not be well known for overseas diplomacy, nor have many friends in Arab lands, but he also has streets names after him in both Tirana & Tbilisi.

Other streets in Pristina are named after Bush's presidential predecessor Bill Clinton and former Czech immigrant Madeleine Albright, the first female US Secretary of State who served under Clinton, in honour of their support during and after the Yugoslav conflict.

Refreshingly plain inside, the cathedral featured a stained-glass window of Saint Teresa standing hand in hand with the other most recent new Saint, Pope John Paul II.

The new age church featured a super-fast lift up its bell tower and for €2 we sped to the top for the best views in town. Despite the drizzle we could see a fair distance.

Having spotted the unusual national library building from on high, we decided that we could tick it off our 'must see' list without needing to trek there in the rain.

There was one other item I wanted to see – the sculpture named Heroinat.

Erected in 2015, the huge face depicted is made up of 20,000 identical discs of that same face. The 20,000 number represents the estimated number of Kosovar women raped during the atrocities of the '90s conflict.

Just let that sink in for a minute. 20,000 victims of an awful crime, who will never ever receive justice in their lives and who will undoubtedly be unable to ever forget their ordeal.

This really harrowing thought made me speechless for a while. Lots of the poor souls will undoubtedly have fallen pregnant too.

That's when I stopped thinking about the unpalatable events, coming around again with the realisation that I was on holiday.

I also took a quick snap of the 'New Born' installation opposite. The installation was unveiled on 17 February 2008, the day that Kosovo formally declared its independence from Serbia.

The monument consists of the English-language word 'NEWBORN' in capital block letters. Originally painted yellow, it was later repainted with the flags of the countries that have recognised Kosovo as an independent nation.

For our visit, the now graffitied monument had been repainted dull grey with the odd patch of brickwork. The 'N' & the 'W' had also been laid flat. We were not sure why but guessed it may have had something to do with commemorating the fall of the Berlin Wall.

After our exertions in the wet, it was time for a dark beer, before returning via Madeleine Albright Street to our hotel and the adjacent pizzeria.

It was to be early to bed for us as we had an early start the next day for our first train journey of the 2017 Balkan tour, Pristina to Skopje.

Annoyingly the bar was right below our room and despite it being empty, the barman was insisting upon playing loud popular music, which now filled our room. Try as I might, I could not get to sleep with my ears trained in to every unpopular track.

After thirty-minutes I could stand it no longer, so re-dressed of sorts and went to politely ask the barman to turn the music down. He readily obliged, only to turn the beatbox onto full blast once more at five next morning as he prepared our breakfast. No need for an alarm clock then!

Despite our 'proximity' to the station, we took a taxi this time to avoid any accidents!

Chapter Ten – Action Stations

🚆Pristina to Hani-I-Elezit Departure 07.10 Arrival 09.05, 70KM

The Kosovo Express

When Pristina was just a moderate city in Yugoslavia it was an outpost on a vast rail network with Belgrade at its hub and major transit points in Zagreb, Skopje, Sarajevo, Ljubljana, Podgorica, Nis & Ploče.

Pristina itself saw trains running to Skopje, Belgrade (via Mitrovica) and throughout Kosovo. Following the break-up of Yugoslavia, the horrendous conflict and Kosovo's self-proclaimed independence from Serbia in 2008, Trainkos was born to run the network in the fledgling nation.

With Serbia not recognising independence and dominating Kosovo's borders, Trainkos did not have many international crossings to manage, save for a line to Skopje.

Sadly, economics has dictated that only the rail route to the Macedonian border remains, including some shuttle runs along part of that same line for domestic purposes.

The rest of the country is served by bus only nowadays as train infrastructure and maintenance does not come cheap and buses are faster and therefore more popular.

Every last cent of public transport money was justifiably ploughed into the building of the hugely impressive Albania-Kosovo Highway that we had travelled on.

With Kosovo being 90% populated by ethnic Albanians, this route was always going to be a priority.

We arrived at 06.40, just in time to see our monster loco, painted in Trainkos red & grey, decoupled from the single passenger carriage and accompanying goods wagon, so it could chug up the track to a run round a loop, back past the carriages and finally around another loop so that it could be rejoined to the train at the other end from whence it had started.

The procedure reads like it was a breathless event, but in reality, the whole procedure took a leisurely fifteen-minutes.

We boarded just before seven and right on time, our friend the station manager donned his red peaked cap, blew his whistle, waved his flag, and we were off on our 70km journey.

We were scheduled to arrive at the border at around nine and were due to be in Skopje before ten.

The carriage interior was pleasingly scruffy, the toilet facilities refreshingly unusable.

We stopped at several stations en route, each manned by a red cap. Stations with names sounding like characters from 'Lord of the Rings', such as Fushlot, Bablak and Stagove came and went as we trundled along purposefully at around 50kmh.

We shared most of the journey with what appeared to be Trainkos retirees. Many wore the uniform of old and they greeted one another like long lost friends.

Their conversation was animated with much laughter, shoulder squeezing and back slapping. They were clearly reminiscing about the good times, maybe times of Yugoslavia under Tito when everything appeared to be stable.

Undoubtedly these aged men in their late sixties plus, would have some sadder tales to tell of conflict, deprivation and fear, but today was not a day for recollection of such, this was 'happy time' recall only.

Each of their lined faces carried a broad smile, a joy to watch for us relative youngsters. The sense of belonging and comradeship is always a great comfort to help in keeping you battling on in times of adversity, convincing yourself that the good times will return.

Back to our progress, we arrived at the small border station right on time, but the waiting connecting train did not appear to be present.

We asked the guard, "iss problem, buss", came his most unwelcome reply. He pointed up the hill, so after taking a few pictures of our train in its new surroundings, this is where me marched.

There was no sign of any bus and nobody seemed to know if, when and where one would appear. There were however plenty of private cars doubling up as taxis. For €15 one would take us the 20km to Skopje.

249

We chose a battered Mercedes and within a minute we were at the border post and still destined to arrive in Skopje just before ten as we had planned. We chose to be dropped at the train station so we could buy our tickets for that nights' overnight adventure to Belgrade.

The train/bus station was the same grim monstrosity that we had frequented eleven years previously. The rest of Skopje had however changed extensively.

A Blot on the Landscape

The new Skopje is not my cup of tea. Imagine having hundreds of millions of euros to invest in improving the infrastructure of your city. You might think about a new train/bus station, improved roads, the introduction of a tram system perhaps.

Imagine instead employing Katie Price, Liberace and Kim Kardashian and asking them to come up with plans on how to turn your city into the envy of other major cities worldwide.

For good measure, you could also indulge them in as many mind-altering drugs as they wanted. The result would probably be very similar to whatever the planners of Skopje have come up with.

Vast Italianate buildings festooned with columns, plinths, statues, frescoes & ornate guttering, grotesque fountains with huge concrete lions belching out water, statue clustered bridges crossing the Vardar River every twenty metres (and another one well on the way to completion).

There were statues featuring breast-feeding women mingled in with armed warriors, giant wooden galleons resting on concrete stilts above the river providing sleeping & dining experiences and several colossal statues towering higher than the buildings, including of course the controversial likeness of Alexander the Great on horseback.

There were so many statues that the Macedonian equivalents of REO Speedwagon, Ben Stiller and Sharon Osbourne must have been honoured in stone.

The planners would have been on a roll (and still continue). That garish 'house' in memory of Mother Teresa that I mentioned before, a ruined castle so renovated that it looks 21st Century and not 6th Century when it was actually built, and perhaps the greatest travesty, the beautification of the old Arabic quarter.

Back on our previous visit in 2006, it had been wonderfully tumbledown with artisan workshops, crooked buildings, a stony network of alleyways and small craft shops.

Now it had shiny marble concrete slabs to walk on, purpose-built jewelers & coffee shops, plus a five-star luxury hotel overlooking a brand-new mosque.

Don't get me wrong, I applaud progress and absolutely agree that every city (especially the capital) should strive to be the best it can possibly be.

What I do not agree with is cramming in more statues than the entire Roman Empire and turning the place into a cross between Vegas, Disneyland and Ebor City.

When I saw they had wedged in an Arc de Triomphe, I started looking round for a Tivoli Fountain and a Taj Mahal!

I understand that a lot of the locals hate the grandiose waste of money (around €1 billion and counting I have heard) and this was certainly in evidence judging by the amount of graffiti sprayed onto only previously perfectly white walls, together with the remains of coloured paint splattered on many of the statues.

I even heard it said that some locals would like another devastating earthquake like the one that flattened the city in 1963. Tongue in cheek of course, but a sure sign of the city's 'Marmite' status with the inhabitants.

We were so pleased that we had visited in '06 when the ancient stone bridge stood in splendid isolation as the only central footbridge spanning the Vardar.

The city needed a facelift back then for sure, but one carried out tastefully and in keeping with its history, not some tacky attempt to outdo the Joneses (or perhaps Belgrade, Zagreb or Ljubljana).

One person's eyesore can make another's heart soar, so if you love the new Skopje, then you are right and I am wrong. Enjoy the spectacle if you are in that camp.

Out & About

Thankfully we arrived armed with a couple of decent things to take in if, as was indeed the case, we wanted to escape the tackiness for a while.

Plans were forged over a very nice dark beer in the spanking new German style brew house. OK, touristic and tacky I know, but when in Rome and at least it wasn't an Irish bar!

After spurning two rip off merchants, we agreed a taxi fare to take us 3km out of town to the village of Vizbegovo see the remains of a Roman aqueduct and then to drive high up into the hills above Skopje, to the St Pantileimon Monastery.

We were soon turning off the highway and along some potholed roads into a rural landscape. Our driver noticeably shuddered as we passed a gypsy camp "Albania mafia," he exclaimed.

As we passed along a dirt track between uncultivated fields, the Roman structure came into view. Although not a hugely impressive example, it still looked well worth our visit.

Upon exiting the taxi, we noticed a photographic drone flying above the wall. A well made up woman was posing for both aerial and land-based cameras.

She was however not dressed like a bride and we couldn't see any groom. It transpired that the black-clad lady in bright red lipstick was a Macedonian pop star diva and was there shooting a vignette for her latest music video.

I hovered just close enough to give me a slight hope that I may appear as an extra on Macedonian MTV!

I chatted to the crew for a few minutes and told them I had been to Skopje eleven years prior and how it had changed so much.

The quip came back that it had changed a lot in the last eleven days!

The aqueduct was in use until the eighteenth century, but only 386 metres and 55 arches of the stone & brick structure remained. It is believed that the aqueduct took water to Skopje from a spring nine kilometres away.

We satisfied ourselves with a few credible shots. It was no Segovia or Caesarea, but definitely a pleasant interlude.

Its presence was completely unmarked in any way and the field was strewn with rubbish and broken glass. We assumed that the structure was perhaps not considered worthy of sightseeing status by the Skopje tourist board, who preferred huge fountains and a multitude of nymph statues. At least officially that is!

We followed Macedonia's Gothic answer to Adele and her crew back down the uneven track to the main road and soon found ourselves spiralling up into the hills above the city.

The monastery complex was situated near the village of Gorno Nerezi on the forested slopes of Mount Vodno, a journey taking about 20-minutes from the centre.

The road up had some very sharp bends and with our driver going like the clappers, we did have our heart in our mouths on occasions. Fortunately, nothing ever came the other way, else the driver's skills and our constitutions could have been severely tested.

The area where the monastery was situated had a refreshing alpine air to it and a wonderful peace. The church dedicated to the saint of health & physicians was a little gem with some lovely frescoed walls & ceiling. I happily paid the €2 entrance fee, for which I received my 'ticket', a postcard depicting the good Saint himself.

Built in the 12th Century, the Byzantine frescoes are famous throughout the Orthodox world.

These included one of Pantileimon, plus others such as depictions of the 'Communion of the Apostles', the 'Transfiguration', the 'Raising of Lazarus', the 'Birth of the Mother of God', the 'Presentation of the Mother of God to the Temple', the 'Entry into Jerusalem' and the 'Descent from the Cross'.

Hamish & I naturally instantly recognised them all (ahem).

I somehow missed the 'no photography' sign and managed to take a few flash free shots before being rebuked!

We were rather reluctant to leave such a lovely area, but after taking in a great view of Skopje far below (infinitely better than close-up), our taxi driver made it clear it was time we descended.

Dropped off in the centre, our driver was absolutely delighted with the €5 tip we gave him. I just wished those who had tried to overcharge us had witnessed it.

I wasted the rest of our stay drinking DB and eating pizza, whilst Hamish had one of his recently acquired dizzy spells, meaning that he had to lay flat out on a bench seat.

We were in the main square and as Hamish dozed and darkness fell, I amused myself by watching the hideous Alexander the Great statue, surrounded by those water belching lion statues, changing colour at regular intervals.

Before long it was time for making off to the train station for our overnight transport to Belgrade.

Hamish was now just about well enough to travel thankfully. If Hamish turns his nose up at a DB, you know that he must be unwell. However, there was nothing like the thought of an overnight train journey to put him into recovery mode and bring a slight spring to his step.

🚂 Skopje to Belgrade Depart 22.14 Arrival 07.42, 322KM

Sleepless in Serbia

No trip around Eastern Europe would be complete without an overnight train journey.

One day there will probably be high speed routes and super modern trains in the region, making slow progress through the night a rarer experience – a huge loss in my opinion.

For now, there are still plenty of opportunities to bunk up for the night in your carriage, being lulled to sleep by the gentle rocking of the train and the tinkling sound of wheel tappers.

The only worrying aspect of our pending journey was that, as had been the case on previous such journeys, we were not able to secure our berth for the journey until we saw the guard on the train shortly before departure.

Our train would start from Thessaloniki in the evening and arrive in Skopje around 10pm. What if all berths were taken? What if we would be crammed in with four others who would be already snoring loudly as we would have to clamber up to the top bunks in the dark?

These and other unsavory thoughts had crossed our minds all day long.

We arrived back at the hideous train/bus station to retrieve our bags in good time on the off chance that we could secure our beds for the night after all.

No chance, the place was virtually deserted aside from a couple of convenience stores, some weary travellers and a few locals who seemed intent on sleeping the night away inside the terminal building.

We had just enough coinage left to buy some Balkan style jaffa cakes, some cheese nachos (old favourites from my inter-rail days and still an essential train journey staple), some bananas and water.

Hamish was famished due to not eating earlier, so he devoured most of his snacks in double quick time.

With me having already drunk three DBs and Hamish having no beer appetite, we unusually did not buy any bottles for the journey, not that we could have afforded any anyway.

We waited for the arrival of our train on the cold, dark platform and only had a couple of drunks for company.

At one point one of them tried to engage in some slurred conversation with us, to which we grunted something along the lines of "we don't understand, we are English you know," before swiftly moving along the platform.

The train and huge diesel locomotive pulled in fifteen minutes late. There is something fabulous about the guttural sound of a great big diesel loco. Not quite up there with the romance of steam and not good for the environment, but another delightful encounter all the same, the like of which you no longer get in the UK.

Two anxious travellers made a rapid beeline for the sleeping compartment. Our anxiety was happily unfounded as we were allocated a six-berth carriage to ourselves for €6 each and were soon happily laying out crisp white sheets on the lower bunks.

What we initially considered as great fortune, soon dissipated, however.

We realised that the heat was on full power as we started to fry. Unfortunately, the on/off slider control had no effect on the temperature. We had two options, move to another carriage or roast.

Just like the heating control however, the train guard refused to yield. He intimated that all carriages were the same and that the full-on heat was controlled centrally with just two settings – off and red hot.

He refused the off option on the basis that it would get cold later.

Like the rogue heating system, we were stuck. What had only moments earlier appeared to be a comfortable journey in the offing, turned into an irritating, sleepless, fractious journey.

I even shouted out "this is absolute b******s!" at one point in the early hours as I struggled to cope with the prickly heat.
To make matters worse, the window refused to open. I immediately thought of Matthew Woodward who had described such a predicament on his trans-Siberian adventure recounted in his excellent book 'Trans-Siberian Adventures'.

I will leave you to take a read of his account, which involves a spanner, a spot of DIY and some sheer panic!

Our route would take us through Niš, infamous of course as the start point of our most tortuous train trip ever in 2006, as we had made our way to Sofia.

Sub-zero temperatures had been the issue back then, the complete opposite of the current predicament. We considered however that the curse of Niš had struck yet again!

I moved to the middle bunk in a vain attempt for some respite and did thankfully at least sleep for a few hours to avoid having to read any 'welcome to Niš' signage (arrival due 03.08).

We had fallen an hour behind schedule during our fitful sleep, scuppering any lingering thoughts we may have had to take a side trip to the beautiful Serbian city of Novi Sad, which we had strongly considered doing before returning to Belgrade and making our way onwards to Timisoara in Romania.

It was now morning, 06.30 to be precise, and a chance to view some of the Serbian countryside slipping by. We stopped in a few small stations, joyfully each stop sending a wheel tapper scurrying over to tap the wheels of the train to sound out whether any may have become damaged since the last station.

Something really tickles me about wheeltappers. I am always reminded of the classic Will Hay film, 'Oh, Mr Porter'.

At the start of the film he his asked why he taps the train wheels, to which he replies, "when it goes clang, I know that the wheel is there and if it doesn't go clang, I know the train has left already."

Back to the present, I also noticed how smart all the stations guards looked in their immaculate uniforms. A far cry from some of the scruffy so and so's serving the UK's Network Rail (you know who you are, East Croydon!).

We finally reached the outskirts of Belgrade, with the usual train graveyards & maintenance stock, plus the now familiar sight of the controversial expensive bridge over the Danube (the Pupin Bridge was finished in December 2014 and cost €260 million to construct, considered a huge waste of money by many Serbs).

We pulled in just before nine, with my impoverished inter-rail days of the late '80s coming flooding back, as I arrived feeling tired, irritated & unwashed.

We would be heading straight off to the Belgrade Dunav Station for our train to Vrsac on the Romanian border, from where we would take another train to Timisoara.

We had no idea where Dunav was, but I was immediately in that unpleasant situation of needing a wash to even think about thinking straight, whilst needing some Serbian coins to gain entry to the less than inviting station toilets, whilst not being able to think straight enough to work out how to get the small amount of currency we may need for our short stay in the Serbian capital.

A vicious circle of dithering!

I was very irritable with it all, but eventually after much deliberation I decided that a wash was priority number one and all else could wait.

I therefore changed €5 at an awful exchange rate in the station bureau de change, bought my way into the dank facilities and washed in freezing cold water as disheveled blokes went through their toilet rituals around me. That was one memory that I hadn't minded leaving firmly in the past!

When I dropped my toothbrush on the bathroom floor, I figured that it would never survive the bacteria attack and promptly binned it, leaving me to clean my teeth with my finger!

Despite the grim nature of the station, I was tinged with sadness to learn that less than a year later it had served its purpose for the last time.

On 30 June 2018 the last train to Budapest left the station at 21:40 after over 130-years of service. International trains were nearly all relocated to the new Prokop Station, the exception being the train to Bar in Montenegro, which relocated to the Topčider railway station.

Back to 2017 and 'Stinky' Hamish had used my ablution time wisely and got information about how to get to Dunav. We could walk 300 metres and catch a bus taking twenty-minutes to get there. I had plenty of money for bus fare, so this is what we decided to do.

After watching two packed rush-hour buses sail through without stopping, we abandoned that idea. Not that getting a taxi was much easier.

I first drew out about €10 worth of local beans, then we flagged down two taxis who had no idea of where Dunav was, before resignedly trudging back to Belgrade Central to try to find a driver who did know. Third time lucky maybe?

After much discussion between the drivers waiting on the rank, we were finally given the thumbs up for a lift. That was just the start of our fun.

We were dropped near the front of the nondescript and decidedly tatty Dunav station building. There was not much clue that it was a station, maybe a sign as to why taxi drivers were seemingly unaware of its presence.

Upon entering the building, our hearts sank. A scrawled note pronounced, 'No Trains Romania'.

The train lady behind the counter was less than helpful, giving us a shoulder shrug and a response of "no train," when asked how we could get to Romania.

We agreed, we would get to Vrsac and chance our arm there. Tickets procured for eighty minutes hence, I now needed to assuage my need for coffee.

There was a shabby looking cafe adjacent to the station and there we headed, more in hope than expectation. As soon as we opened the door to the dingy place, we were hit with a wall of oily food aromas mixed with thick cigarette smoke.
Someone approached us from the dark depths, but we did not have time to see who it was as we shut the door and scarpered.

After a few minutes, we found a bakery selling pastries & sandwiches. Unfortunately for Hamish all the fresh sarnies contained ham, leaving him to consume a cheese pie soaked in grease. My cheese & ham roll was very tasty in contrast.

As the pie weighed heavily on Hamish's stomach, we were pointed in the direction of a coffee shop. The pleasant place did a lovely latte, had an immaculate bathroom for a second all together more refreshing wash and power points to recharge our phones.

Things were looking up!

🚆 Belgrade Dunav to Vrsac Departure 12.08 Arrival 13.48, 73KM

Romanian Holiday

We boarded our shiny new electric train and were soon heading north-east for the hundred-minute journey.

The train was full of locals going about their normal business, made up entirely of students & pensioners heading out of the capital back to their towns & villages.

I asked one of the younger travellers if she knew how we could get to Timisoara. Neither she or her friends could help unfortunately.

As well as the train debacle, I had also had to contend with my first ever Airbnb issue. The owner of the flat we had booked had suddenly become incommunicado, until at the last minute he texted back bleating about water leaks and related damage.

Suspiciously he asked me to cancel on Airbnb's website for a full refund. I however smelt a rat and the website terms & conditions confirmed that if I cancelled at short notice, all payments would be forfeit.

I sent Airbnb a screenshot photo of the rogue owner's text and eventually secured not only a full refund but compensation too. Nice people at Airbnb!

I also managed to book a very good replacement, so at least that potential drama had been negated.

We didn't seem so lucky once we arrived in Vrsac. There were no taxis, no buses, we were 3km from the centre and our second unhelpful Serb rail lady of the day did not know how to phone us a taxi!

We went outside hoping that something would come up. We clearly looked like lost sheep as a chap approached us to ask what we were doing.

As luck would have it, he had a taxi driver friend who he called and agreed to take us to Romania for €50. We saw our saviour leave and waited patiently.

Quicker than expected our taxi arrived. He confirmed he could take us for €50, but we did find it a little strange when he phoned his mum to fish out his passport, which he would collect on the way.

When a second taxi turned up it dawned on us what has happened. We were in the wrong taxi!

The younger driver acceded to the elder's curt demand that he hand-over his rightful lucrative fare.

He then proceeded to snatch our bags out of the boot of the other taxi and stick them in his, just in case there was any further disagreement.

I felt sorry for our clearly disappointed driver. He had lost a decent earner and who knows maybe a good time in Timisoara.

I handed him my last Serbian currency (about €3 worth), and he at least managed half a smile in return.

We were on our way at last. The jolly border guard called me William Shakespeare after flicking through my passport, before cheerily welcoming us to Romania. We passed the car boot inspection and were on our way in minutes.

It wasn't so easy for the Eastern European lorry drivers. The queue at the border of the EU was at least three miles long, as every truck was meticulously inspected by the Romanian authorities. This could well be the same in Dover & Calais post BREXIT I thought. Yuk!

What compels anybody to be a lorry driver is beyond me, but I guess they feel the same abhorrence when thinking about office work.

After about 45-minutes since leaving the border, we were pulling up in a leafy suburb outside our accommodation, 20-minutes' walk from the centre of the delightful city of Timisoara.

So, after eight late September days away from the UK, we had arrived in the sixth and final country of our mini-tour of the region. Had we left the best to last? On balance, we probably had.

First up our accommodation. I promised the lovely hostess Miriana that I would write about her on my blog and six weeks later I finally got around to it!

It was clear from the outset that Miriana was very friendly and extremely proud & knowledgeable about her city & country. A veritable tourist information centre, Miriana explained that Timisoara was the first place in Europe to get electric street lights and horse-drawn trams.

Our spacious & modern apartment was set in a lovely walled garden full of flowers, plants and vines dripping with fruit. We were even invited to help ourselves if we wanted any grapes!

We had the best part of two days left of our trip and were to be bathed in sunshine for both days, a nice change from the three days of constant drizzle in Kosovo.

We found Timisoara was a delightful small city, easily explored on foot. If like me you like a ride for the hell of it in rattily old trams, you are well catered for in that department too.

It is a university city and the students add a vibrant, laid-back feel to the place.

It was the students and the permanent inhabitants who started the protests in Romania that eventually saw the fall and execution of the feared & despised Ceausescu family, who had ruled the country with an iron fist for much of its history behind the Iron Curtain.

Our accommodation was situated a pleasant stroll from the River Bega and the unusual looking main cathedral with its green a gold turrets and gingerbread brickwork.

The cathedral fronted onto the first of three fabulous squares, all of which we saw on our first night and looked forward to seeing in the daylight.

After drawing out some Romanian beans, we ate in a very lively outdoor café on the furthest square. Next day we were to retrace our steps by daylight.

First up was Victoriei Square, adorned by very nice gardens and many tumbledown buildings oozing character. The Orthodox cathedral sat at one end and the opera house at the other, like two ornate bookends.

We walked past all the inviting cafes and headed for the opera house coffee shop, where we were to sit in the sunshine watching the world go by. I was tempted to visit the opera to buy tickets to see Aida but thought I would save a visit for a romantic future trip with Mrs Wilbur.

Next up a stone's throw away stood Libertății Square, also known as Parade Platz by locals due to its former because military role.

The imposing Town Hall was the stand-out building of the cobbled square, which also was location for several statues, including an ancient stone one of St Mary and a modern ironwork one of a see-through boy holding an imaginary mobile phone.

It was a place for old men to hang out and parents & grandparents to wheel their kids around. The balloon sellers and candy floss stall were doing a brisk trade.

The square was also a main tram thoroughfare and indeed we rattled through it ourselves a couple of times. It was also home to the unusual West City Radio building, architecturally a cross between Gaudi & Wren.

In a recurring theme, we saved the best until last. The Baroque Unirii Square was dominated by the Catholic Cathedral and Serbian Orthodox Cathedral placed opposite to each other.

The present square was completed in the late 18th century. During the course of its entire 300-year history, Unirii Square was the focal point of religious events, military parades and other events of political and cultural importance.

The square's main architectural style was Baroque that combined beautifully with the classic & 1900's style.

Besides the two churches, there was also the Baroque Palace, whose construction began in the middle of the 18th century and now housed the art museum of Timisoara.

The building is a mix of the Baroque and Rococo styles, living in perfect harmony with the other buildings.

On the west pediment of the square was the residence of the Serbian Orthodox Bishop, whose facade was remodeled between 1904 and 1905 in a style closer to the Serbian national style by the Hungarian architect Székely.

The square as a whole was up there with the best ones in Prague, Vienna, Budapest & Bratislava in my opinion. Not only that but it also had some lovely bars & restaurants. We ate & drank heartily without hurting the budget too much.

That evening we ate in the same restaurant and even had the same meal and DB. A case 'if it ain't broke don't fix it' rather than a reluctance to experiment.

Next morning, I arranged to meet Hamish in the centre as I had a Saturday business call to make. We planned to dart about on the trams a bit, to take in the train station and finish with some DB in the sunshine.

When we met up ninety-minutes later, Hamish informed me that he had got hopelessly lost. Despite us having made the walk together twice before, he managed to follow the wrong set of tram lines and ended up in a residential area.

Realising his mistake he retraced his steps, which meant that he had arrived at our rendezvous point only five minutes before me.

I rest my case for the worst sense of direction in Europe award!

We bought some tram tickets and headed off to the train station to photograph some locos and the general goings on (I am not a train-spotter, honest!).

After thirty-minutes of train related fun, we clambered aboard a really ancient tram that would take us to Libertăţii Square.

From there we took the short walk to Unirii Square where we took up residence in an outdoor bar. The relaxed bar staff were quite happy for drinkers to venture next door for a takeaway salad.

I offered to get the salads, whilst Hamish ordered the DBs. Unfortunately, I nearly 'poisoned' my buddy as the apple & cheese salad also contained bacon, unbeknown to me.

After spitting out a mouthful into a serviette, I was duty-bound to give Hamish my tuna salad in exchange for his almost complete one. Sorry mate!

The Silva DBs soon had him forgetting his ordeal however, before we had to reluctantly leave our wonderful DB drinking in the sunshine as we had a plane to catch that Saturday afternoon.

Another top trip in the Balkans had been had. It simply never fails to deliver.

Bonus Chapter – Balkan Holidays

In the mid-to-late '90s, my good pal Lang worked in London for a travel company who specialised in holidays in Bulgaria and some neighbouring Balkan countries.

This gave me some fantastically discounted holidays - three summer package vacations on the Bulgarian Black Sea and two ski holidays in the Rila Mountains, with change from £300 for the lot.

The beach holidays were pretty wild affairs and much of what went on is best left to the old adage, 'what goes on tour, stays on tour.'

Aeroplane Food

Like most beach holidays of the like they tend to blur into each other, just like James Bond movies. Even the resort names were pretty nondescript – two visits to Golden Sands (GS) and one to Sunny Beach (SB).

The first one to GS in 1993 when aged 28 was probably the most riotous. We went as a three with Hamish.

The whole trip was hilarious from start to finish. We flew with Balkan Air in an archaic Tupolev Turbo Prop. The flight was hairy and the in-flight food even hairier.

We devised a game for the weeklong break. Hamish would be judge and he could award points to singletons Lang and I for outrageous acts, drinking feats etc. There was nothing to trouble

'Dirty Sanchez' or even a Channel 5 'pukeumentary', but the dares were outlandish enough for us.

It was up to Lang and me to suggest dares and Hamish would let us know in advance how many points they would earn, from one to three.

The loser of the game was condemned to eat the whole in flight meal on the way home - that was some incentive I can tell you!

Bulgaria '93 was just coming to terms with the fall of communism and much of the infrastructure and culture were very much of the communist times.

Indeed, GS and its sister resort SB were places where the stand out comrades of the Communist Party and the most productive workers went as a reward for their endeavours.

The resort did have a lovely sandy beach, flanked by some monstrous grey concrete hotels and one English pub, The Golden Lion.

Lang was determined that it wouldn't be him eating on the flight home, earning decent points for kissing a horse's bottom, wiping his face in a full plate of spaghetti Bolognese in a restaurant, approaching a stunning girl and telling her all his O-level results, asking a barman for his autograph (and getting it) and more.

GS was just thirty-minutes away from the strategic Black Sea port of Varna and with my love of ports we travelled there to spend a few hours away from the beach.

There were some US navy frigates in - we were to meet many of their crew in GS that same night in the clubs and bars, notably the Red Lobster strip club. where several of their members were ejected for being drunk & disorderly.

It was baking hot and we paid a visit to Varna train station. The station itself was a scruffy, dusty affair and just looking at the rusty old carriages sweltering in the heat brought back memories of some of the less pleasant inter-rail experiences.

On another day we booked a boat trip to go fishing. On the trip we met a larger than life Bavarian character named Wolfgang, who now resided in GS for six months of the year.

The boat trip was notable for one thing only. Before anybody had a chance to cast a line, we were heading back to shore. This was after Hamish and I had already delayed the start by fifteen minutes due to going to the incorrect departure pier.

The reason we headed back? Hamish was violently seasick! This was rather embarrassing as you can imagine as I was compelled to declare our friendship as I helped him off the vessel. Lang had done well to forego the opportunity.

The first he found out about the incident was when he read the excursion agent's report explaining why the vessel owner was claiming extra payment for additional fuel due to the unplanned return to shore to drop off a sick passenger. This meant that the trip was now loss making for Balkan Holidays.

When Lang found out that the invalid passenger was Hamish, he absolutely wet himself with laughter. We also bumped into Wolfgang later who revealed that nobody had caught a thing after they went back out and they had all been given a bunch of grapes to compensate. He then did a very passable impression of Hamish being ill!

Lang won the points game. I gave up after he went paragliding blindfolded. He was far too determined. However, I pulled a fast one by requesting a vegetarian meal for the journey home - this consisted of two apples and an orange, which I was more than happy to eat!

Men Behaving Badly

In '95 it was Sunny Beach for Lang and me only. The second week of the trip was to be in the Turkish resort of Buyukcekmekhe. This entailed a ten-hour coach transfer, with the coach leaving at midnight.

Like an idiot, I decided that the same night was a good occasion to get totally plastered, which I put totally down to meeting two female Irish nurses, who enticed me back to their hotel room (nothing worthy of any points though)!

I totally lost track of time as the beers and lilt of the nurse's accent had made me feel rather dreamy. The girls were drunker than I was and the youngest named Brenda had fallen asleep still holding a beer. Caroline happened to ask what time my coach was leaving. 'Shit, shit and shit again, ten minutes ago!'

I hardly had time to say goodbye before I was tearing out of the hotel room and down the six flights of stairs to the ground floor. We had to check our cases in earlier with the holiday rep, so all my clothes would be on the bus by now. Surely it would not leave without me?

I could not hack another week in SB and had visions of having to buy clothes and toiletries and find a new hotel (though I was fairly confident Irish hospitality would have helped me out in that department).

As I burst out of the hotel, I literally bumped into an anxious looking Lang. His less than friendly greeting consisted of one word, "Twat!"

I was still very drunk as I clumsily followed his lead before staggering aboard. Rather than being sheepish and embarrassed, I just kept saying sorry in between hiccups.

There were only seven of us on the fifty-two-seat coach. I made straight for the back seat and sprawled out, very soon to be snoring my head off. I was not at my best when awoken at five in the morning for border control.

This meant getting off the coach, queuing for various papers and stamps, handing over a pristine £5 note (apparently a crumpled note would see you refused admittance) and finally receiving your entry visa.

The whole process took two hours, not a healthy position for somebody in the early stages of a crashing hangover.

I noticed some withering looks from my fellow passengers as I clambered back on the bus. Lang helpfully explained that I had kept everybody awake with my snoring, on top of the fact that I had caused his frantic search for my drunken self, which had delayed the departure. Oops, how to win friends and influence people!

At around eight we stopped for breakfast at a dilapidated roadside café. It was already 20C+ and airless. The food on offer was greasy stewed lamb, mushy greens, butter beans swimming in olive oil and chickpeas, all garnished with the odd dead fly.

It was enough to make the strongest stomachs turn and I suddenly realised how Hamish had felt on that fishing trip a few years before. I needed to find a toilet and quickly. Our holiday rep ushered me outside to a wooden hut containing three stinking cubicles.

It was empty apart from a few dozen living flies. I was soon losing all that beer that I had consumed the night before so avidly. It actually made the squat loo smell better - I will spare you the finer details but there were more deposits evident in there than an average bank gets in a week!

I felt a whole lot better afterwards however and celebrated with a breakfast choc-ice, once I had worked out that 14,000 Turkish Lire = £1.

The Mediterranean resort was pleasant enough, but I had decided to use it as a gateway to visit Istanbul every day, around an hour away by bus.

The magnificent seven all stayed in the same hotel and as we were the only Brits there, we were expected to eat together. We therefore got to know each other pretty quickly. Stanley (a double for Charles Hawtrey), his skittish wife Shirley and their thirteen-year-old (going on six) son Stanley Junior, were from Yorkshire. Pete and Di were a quiet couple in their mid-fifties from Surrey.

The first thing we did was to make it clear that Lang and I were not a couple. Shirley then christened me 'Snore Pig' and the name stuck for the rest of the trip.

Lang had a load of Balkan Holiday baseball caps that became known as currency as they were readily accepted by hotel staff as payment for beer. He became quite a celebrity during our stay and was even asked to play tambourine for the resident band at the hotel nightclub!

I did make it to Istanbul on four of the five full days we stayed at the resort. Lang accompanied me on the first three days. We stepped into the chaos that was Topkapi Bus Station. The place was wonderful and desperate at the same time.

Buses from all over Turkey descended there. The Izmir Express, Ankara Flyer, Bodrum Rapide and Aegean Sea Bus vied with regional buses like ours and dozens and dozens of minibuses.

Every vehicle showed signs of a scrape or two and without exception all of their windscreens were cracked. Our bus even had its nearside wing mirror taped on!

The exhaust fumes were choking, yet the bus station was home to a thriving community of traders, buskers, beggars, water-sellers, hotel touts, taxi drivers, purveyors of lotto tickets and just general hangers on.

There were food stands everywhere with swarthy men stirring huge vats of stew and rice, old grey-haired men barbecuing corn on the cob and others cycling around with baskets stacked high with ring doughnut style bread covered in sesame seeds (known as simit in those parts).

Apart from the ladies covered from top to toe getting on and off buses, this was a totally male domain. Even the shops flanking the bus depot selling everything from nylons to neon and bootleg CDs to fake designer watches, were fronted by men only.

I shuddered when an elderly chap bought a peach and ate it in about thirty seconds. No doubt he had consumed a fair amount of lead deposits with the wrinkled fruit!

Lang and I decided we would take a taxi to Topkapi Palace and agreed a fee of around £2. We soon arrived after around fifty pence worth of journey and handed over the agreed fee. Unbelievably the scheming taxi driver demanded the same fee from each of us.

Upon refusing, the doors were locked centrally and the argument threatened to turn ugly with the crook driver claiming he would take us to see his friends if we did not pay. Reluctantly we did so with all the grace of a Neanderthal. What a bastard!!!!

A carpet shop owner soon stopped (accosted) us, as he "would be honoured to show us his wares." We had a free Turkish coffee for our trouble but left the shop empty handed despite the owner's best attempts to convince us to make a purchase of "the finest silk kilims in Istanbul." I was still spitting out coffee granules an hour later.

We visited the fantastic palace that made us forget about our rip off taxi and over the next few days we took in the Blue Mosque, the Ayasofya Mosque, Grand Bazaar (where Lang bartered for those white socks), underground cisterns and took a ferry across the Bosporus to Asia.

It's a Drag

The following Winter I went skiing for the first time, accompanying Lang to the Bulgarian resort of Borovets.

Surprisingly there was even more detail here that must stay unwritten than the GS trip, suffice to say that Lang excelled himself with the après ski!

I was known as Mr. Bean on ice within my ski-school for my skiing prowess. To be fair, my skiing was OK, but my clumsy self could not get to grips with the draglifts, falling off constantly.

The stress of queuing up for ages, grabbing a pole with dozens of people watching and then experiencing the excruciating humiliation of coming a cropper part way up was palpable.

The masses would gawp and laugh, whispering smart remarks as I was lambasted by my ski instructor. This all made me shiver with fear as I approached any ski lift and has left an indelible scar on my memory ever since.

At the time, the humiliation I felt was only matched by the exultation & relief when I finally made it to the top!

On one occasion a chap dressed as ALF, the acronym of US children's comedy character Alien Life Form, helped me to my feet after one all too common crash landing. I was pictured with him after the helping hand, much to Lang's amusement.

I was pretty pleased when it was too foggy one day to ski. We took the opportunity to take the long minibus journey to the splendid Rila Monastery high up in the Rila Mountains. It was well worth the five-hour round trip.

On my second ski holiday Hamish joined us. We all went gratis, as Hamish was official photographer for the following season's brochure.

In my ski-school were two attractive, albeit bimbo, Brummie girls that we christened the Trouts. They were to act as the primary models for the brochure shots, posing in skiwear, swimwear and nightclub wear. Fifteen years later they still featured in the brochure and as far as I am aware, they still do today!

There was one notable nightclub come strip club called Big Apple. This featured some exotic dancers, some singers, a magician and some strippers. It was quite a cabaret, which we were to see four times, all in the interest of some good photos for the brochure of course!

One evening, the cheap cocktails got the better of Lang and I and we got up on stage and started to strip. Hamish managed to get two photos before security intervened!

On the penultimate day of the trip I had an incident that was to prove to be my last ever day on skis. We had graduated to a Red run, Black in places. We had arrived by gondola, so no ski lift dramas thankfully and I was feeling pretty pleased with myself as I skied to the bottom without incident.

What I did not know was that there was no lower gondola meaning that the only option to get back up was a hideous draglift. Not only was it a steep incline needing immaculate balance to stay on, but half way up there was a wooden ramp and bridge that you had to ski over whilst holding onto the lift pole with one hand and your own ski poles with the other.

This was mission impossible for me, as I approached the ramp my whole body froze with fear and part way up my skis crossed, off I came falling five feet onto the snow and then sliding and rolling down from whence I had come, my head just inches away from the concrete and metal of the ramp's struts as I tumbled down the mountain.

I eventually landed in a heap at the bottom, taking a minute or two to come to my senses. Jürgen the German instructor came racing over, concern in his voice, to shout out an inquiry as to my well-being.

To my (and his) relief I was physically OK, but mentally I was finished with skiing. Jürgen tried to urge me to continue, stating that I could do it, that I should get back on the bike, how he would help me. No Fucking Way!!!!

This left me with no option but to walk up the mountain with my skis and poles (thoughtfully retrieved by Jürgen from various parts of the slope). Furthermore, the middle gondola station was out of action meaning that my upward journey was two kilometres away!

To my mind this was preferable to the bridge structure, as dizzying thoughts of concrete plinths and my near-death experience came flashing before my eyes.

I waited until Jürgen was out of sight before I started my lonely, energy-sapping trudge up the mountain, stopping to look at the bridge and thinking what might have been when I saw the concrete and steel once more. I froze transfixed to the spot for several minutes and shuddered!

I swore profoundly and audibly as I passed the non-functioning gondola. I was positively apoplectic a few metres later when I went arse over tit and watched my skis slide back down the mountain.

Fortunately, there was a plateau about twenty-five metres down where my skis now rested a few feet apart. I begrudged every one of those extra fifty metres there and back. If they had slid the whole one kilometre back down I would have left the sodding things and wouldn't have cared less about the fine!

Eventually I got to the top after about ninety minutes of effort. Quite honestly it was one of the most physically draining things I had ever done, right up there with school cross-country running.

I had stitch and felt sick, but thankfully held it all together as my ski group waved at me from their lunch table.

Despite my red face, I joined them. The Trouts both kissed me on the cheek when I recounted my experience. Jürgen said how worried he had been and had expected to be coming down the mountain with me in a rescue helicopter. That thought made me feel a whole lot better!

I waved the group farewell as they skied back down the mountain. I would see Karen and Sharon (the Trouts) later, having grown fond of the daft pair.

I bought a lunch of steak and chips and a glass of red - I thought that was the least I deserved in the circumstances. As I sat there waiting for my food to arrive, I realised for the first time the majesty of my surroundings.

I had been so pumped up and wound up before, that I had been oblivious to it. Now the pressure was off - no more draglifts, no more Germanic ear bashing, no more anxiety and no more red face (at least until I made an unwanted pass at Karen that evening that was!).

The sky was indigo blue with just a few wispy white clouds; the sun shone brightly and made the pristine snow sparkle; the rugged mountains thrust skywards, their snow-capped peaks glinting invitingly; snow covered fir forests stood motionless bordering the ski slope, that were filled with multi-coloured winter sports enthusiasts; bouts of laughter, chatter and the odd playful scream floated on the air; a hovering eagle cast its broad shadow as it stared out its potential prey; a family of Canada geese swept gracefully past with a coordinated honk to mark the occasion.

If only I could paint, I thought to myself.

An air of tranquility came over me; the world was a wonderful place again. Even the leathery steak could not spoil my mood. If this was to be my last ever ski experience, it was fine by me I concluded.

Picture Gallery

Lake Ohrid Fisherman, 2006

Getting Cold on the Nis to Sofia Train, 2006

Tirana Toy Tiger Entrepreneur, 2007

Albanian Loco in Durres, 2007

Montenegro Loco in Bar, 2007

Kotor, Montenegro, 2007

Meteora, Greece, 2006

Dubrovnik, Croatia, 2007

Mostar Diving Club, 2007

Lake Ohrid, 2006

Alexander Nevsky Cathedral, Sofia 2012

Spielfeldstrasse Station, 1987

Belgrade Main Station, 2012

Belgrade Dunav Station, 2017

Split, Croatia 2012

That Infamous Bridge in Sarajevo, 2012

Old Stone Bridge, Skopje, 2006

Main Square, Skopje, 2017

Heroinat Monument, Pristina, 2017

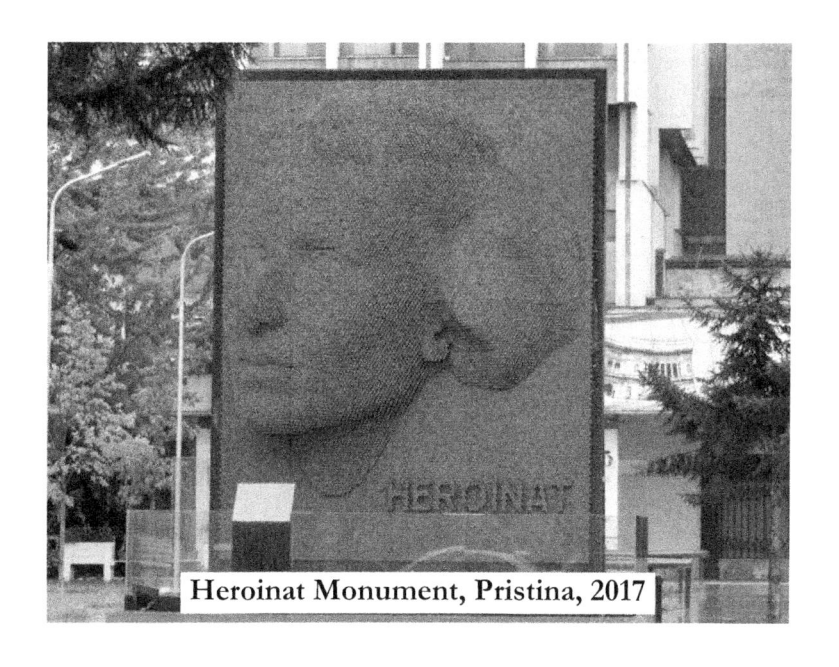

Aqueduct, Skopje, 2017

Kosovar Train, Hani-I-Elezit, 2017

Sarajevo Tram, 2012

Will & ALF, 1996

Skanderbeg Square, Tirana, 2007

Ljubljana Dragon, 2017

Greece-Macedonia Border, 2006

Reflections

The Balkans have been very good to me. My wife is Greek and my travels in the region have been full of wonder, laughter and an all-round fabulous experience.

I have visited and travelled by train in every Balkan nation and have found each one to be vibrant, exciting and great fun.

Tensions are never far below the surface though as you will have read.

The whole Albania-Kosovo-Serbia dispute will never fully disappear, Bosnia is still a nation divided by race & religion, the whole Macedonia issue will not blow away easily, Greece will never truly forgive & forget several centuries of barbaric rule under the Ottoman Turks and throughout the region there are many other disputed territories.

I sincerely hope that a lid can be kept on these volatile lands so that people live in peaceful harmony and travellers can enjoy this most beguiling of regions as I have been so lucky to do.

Glossary of Terms

DB — Dark Beer – the favourite Eastern Europe tipple of Hamish & I

LP — Lonely Planet – our guidebook of choice since Indonesia in 1997

TC — Thomas Cook Timetable – the complete book of train times in Europe and beyond and the second most wonderful book in the world after an atlas!

OPD — One Pound Dares – ridiculous juvenile wagers that would never ever be taken up by anybody with an iota of intelligence

Dark Beer Ratings

#	Name	Country	Score
1	Nikšićko	Montenegro	10
2	Korça	Albania	9
3	Sarajevska Pivara	Bosnia	9
4	Laško Zlatorog	Slovenia	8.5
5	Stolichno	Bulgaria	8
6	Silva	Romania	8
7	Velebitsko	Croatia	8
8	Corfu Dark	Greece	7.5
9	Fix	Greece	7.5
10	Ariana	Bulgaria	7
11	EFES	Turkey	7
12	Skopsko Temno	Macedonia	7

Balkan Train Journeys (overnight journeys in bold)

MM/YY	Start	End	KM	Time
Sept/87	Spielfieldstraß	Maribor – Return	32	0.35
Oct/06	**Istanbul**	**Thessaloniki**	**508**	**14.05**
Oct/06	Thessaloniki	Kalabaka - Return	470	6.16
Oct/06	Thessaloniki	Skopje	199	3.01
Oct/06	Skopje	Niš	205	5.01
Nov/06	Niš	Sofia	163	10.05
Oct/07	Tirana	Durres - Return	72	2.03
Oct/07	Tirana	Shkodra	98	3.27
Oct/07	Bar	Podgorica	56	0.56
Sept/12	**Zagreb**	**Split**	**435**	**8.50**
Sept/12	Ploče	Sarajevo	194	4.53
Sept/12	Sarajevo	Belgrade	330	8.43
Sept/12	**Belgrade**	**Sofia**	**401**	**13.14**

MM/YY	Start	End	KM	Time
Sept/12	Sofia	Gorna Oryakhovitsa – Return	588	8.28
Feb/17	Ljubljana	Skofja Loka – Return	40	1.00
Sept/17	Pristina	Hani-I-Elezit	70	1.55
Sept/17	**Skopje**	**Belgrade**	**322**	**10.25**
Sept/17	Belgrade	Vrsac	73	1.40

About the Author

Will developed a passion for writing from the moment when aged five he was awarded a gold star for his summary account of Peter & The Wolf.

He progressed to have dozens of travel & sport related articles published, before fulfilling an ambition of having his first book commissioned in 2012.

Travel & football are his twin passions and as at 2018 he has travelled to 70 countries, in many of which he has also taken in a top-flight football match.

Travelling around and between countries by train is also a particularly favourite thing for Will to do, with an overnight journey complete with dining car experience being his absolute top-notch travel experience.

You can catch up on Will's global travels on his website at www.wilburstravels.com or his Twitter account @wilburstravels

Coming Next

Wilbur's Travels Part Two will be journeys behind the former Iron Curtain featuring adventures in Belarus, Czechoslovakia, East Germany, Estonia, Hungary, Latvia, Lithuania, Moldova, Poland, Romania, Russia & Ukraine.

'With about ninety-minutes remaining of our mammoth 27-hour journey from Sevastopol to Lviv, an announcement instructed passengers to bring their bedding to the end of the carriage.

We didn't understand a word of course, but as everybody rose in unison, bundled their sheets, blanket and pillowcases together and carried them towards the large lady (a Hattie Jacques lookalike from the film 'Carry on Nurse'), dressed in starched white uniform, white peaked cap and the sort of slippers given away free at up-market hotels, who stood open armed at the end of carriage, we quickly got the message.

We followed suit but encountered a problem. Hamish could not locate his pillow so had no pillowcase to return. Hattie J was counting everything in and demanded to know where my mates' pillowcase was.

Again, we did not understand the demands but knew instantly what the problem was and that it presented an issue for us (him).

There were at least ten people behind us now straining under the weight of their bundles that included thick heavy blankets.

It was Hamish's turn to feel eyes piercing into his person. He could only go bright red and shrug his shoulders. I really hoped that this body language universally meant 'I don't know' rather than being some sort of insult in Ukraine.

In any case, Hamish was commanded to stand aside and wait. He understood the hand signals and imperative tone perfectly and obeyed instantly.

Taking pity on my friend, I joined him in waiting. The expressions of the fellow passengers as they handed in their bedding were unforgiving.

I wondered whether in previous times Hamish's crimes could have led to a spell in some Siberian salt mines. You would have thought so by the stern looks that were now pointed in our direction.

The rest of the bedding was counted in without incident and Hattie then beckoned us to follow her to our seat.

When there she bellowed to our section companions, clearly demanding to know who had the missing pillow……'

To be continued

Printed in Great Britain
by Amazon